SUCCESSFUL INTERVIEWING FOR COLLEGE SENIORS

Library of Congress Cataloging-in-Publication Data

Shingleton, John D.
   Successful interviewing for college seniors / John D. Shingleton.
     p.   .cm.
   ISBN 0-8442-4149-0
   1. Employment interviewing. 2. Vocational guidance. I. Title.
HF5549.5.I6S37   1992
658.14—dc20   91-45143
                                        CIP

Published by VGM Career Horizons, a division of NTC Publishing Group.
© 1992 by NTC Publishing Group, 4255 West Touhy Avenue,
Lincolnwood (Chicago), Illinois 60646-1975 U.S.A.
Manufactured in the United States of America.

2 3 4 5 6 7 8 9 ML 9 8 7 6 5 4 3 2 1

SUCCESSFUL INTERVIEWING FOR COLLEGE SENIORS

JOHN D. SHINGLETON

VGM Career Horizons
a division of *NTC Publishing Group*
Lincolnwood, Illinois USA

About the Author

John D. Shingleton served as Placement Director at Michigan State University for over 25 years, advising thousands of students and alumni on their careers. He founded the Collegiate Employment Research Institute and served as director for many years. He has worked for the Ford Motor Company and the Detroit Edison Company, and he currently is a consultant to numerous universities and corporations primarily on the subject of employment.

He has written extensively on the subject of employment including four other books. He has written a careers column for the Detroit *Free Press* for many years. He has written numerous articles for the *College Placement Journal* and the *College Placement Annual*.

He has received the prestigious Applied Research Award named in his honor by the Midwest College Placement Association. In 1987 he received the Outstanding Professional award from the College Placement Council.

He currently is a member of the Board of Trustees at Michigan State University.

Acknowledgments

I am especially grateful to the students and employers with whom I have worked in this field of career planning and placement. They have taught me much that is included in this book.

A special thanks to Judy Sabatino for compiling and typing the manuscript.

A special pat on the back to Dr. Patrick Scheetz, Director of the Collegiate Employment Research Institute at Michigan State University, for his reviewing the manuscript and offering his able advice.

Constance Rajala, editor, and Kathy Siebel, associate editor, of VGM Career Horizons, also have contributed greatly to this book, for which I am most appreciative.

Thanks also to my wife, Helen, for her suggestions and editing.

John D. Shingleton

Preface

So many graduating seniors, faced with leaving college and entering the world of work, are concerned about what to expect when they begin interviewing for their first job after college. Some realize the importance of the interview, some don't. Regardless, the interview is a turning point in their lives. As with any adventure, no one quite knows what to expect and how to cope with it.

This book covers the job interview from A to Z and can enhance your job potential considerably by helping you understand what you are looking for and how to get it.

Graduating from an institution of higher learning puts you in a special group in terms of what your future can be. Of course, what it can be and what it will be are two different things. You have the educational background and have been provided opportunities to gain experiences that will serve you well in the future.

The problem many seniors have when entering the job market lies in not recognizing they are in a very competitive situation. Employer representatives receive countless resumes, interview on several campuses, and talk to many candidates before making a decision to hire a person. In the more desirable companies, the employer may screen resumes and interviews of anywhere from 10 to 100 candidates seeking a position in the company.

Very often the difference between the person hired and the person rejected is not who is the better candidate but who is better prepared for the interview. Careers can be made and lost at that point alone. You need to spend the time and effort which will enable you to be better prepared than the competition. Recognize this and you will enhance your employability considerably.

The issue before you now, as a graduating senior, is to present your education and your experiences in the best way possible to those employers who have an interest in a person with your qualifications. Having so many credits, courses or degrees doesn't necessarily add up to getting the position or career path you seek. You must be able to present your abilities, knowledge, insight, and personality in a way that will maximize your potential to find the slot that best suits your needs.

Being able to understand the importance of the employment interview and then to present yourself through your interviews in a successful way opens the door for infinite possibilities. The skill with which you handle the interview can have a tremendous impact on how successful you are in your job.

There is an art to the successful interview. Take the time to understand the importance of the interview. This book speaks to helping you maximize your potential when you interview for a position. Plan your interviews and give them a lot of thought—don't just drift with the current and let chance determine your future. Successful interviews can lead to successful lives. Work affects you socially, psychologically, physically, mentally and economically. The job interview is the gateway to the world of work. Make the most of it. Good luck.

John D. Shingleton

To the memory of my mother and father.
Their values are the cornerstone of my life.

Contents

chapter one

The Concept of the Interview and Its Importance

An interview is the crown jewel of a job campaign. If you don't convert employment interviews into job offers, all other efforts are wasted. You make it or lose it in the interview. Thus it is of utmost importance that you prepare properly for the interview. This requires careful analysis of your past achievements, your current situation, and your anticipated preferences. Set aside the time to fix this information clearly in mind before you begin interviewing.

Advance Planning

Among the details needed before a job interview are a summary of your academic preparation, your prior work experiences, a description of the career you expect to pursue, the general category of organization you would like to join, and the preferred geographical area for your desired work.

Before pursuing prospective employers and getting interviews, other preparation is also needed to conduct an effective job campaign. Among the steps necessary for this achievement are: creating a creditable resume, researching various employers that may interest you, understanding the job market and your competition, clarifying your financial expectations, identifying the specific employers you want to interview, gathering all the information you need to sell yourself effectively and identifying your references. Also important is an understanding of the various sources to obtain interviews, i.e., the placement office of your school, faculty contacts, friends who know of job leads, and a variety of other sources. You will, in addition, want to prepare a log of your interviews so you can check the status and results of those interviews at any given time.

Fundamentals

Preparation for the interview consists of three fundamental components. *First*, you must know yourself—your pluses and minuses—very well. And more important, you must be able to articulate who and what you are. Part of the preparation for an interview should include practicing your answers to certain questions. More will be included on that later, however.

Second, you must know your prospective employer and the anticipated job opening. You should know as many details as possible about the employers and the jobs you are seeking: the product line, profitability, organizational structure, employment locations, reputation of the employer and the potential for advancement. The more knowledge you have about an employer, the more you can command the interview. You also can tailor your answers to questions the prospective employer is asking.

Third, you must know your competition and your bargaining position. To assume you have all the answers and qualifications that will guarantee you a job puts you at a great disadvantage. It is much better to assume there will always be someone better prepared and qualified. This will make you try harder. Being knowledgeable about the whole job search strategy can greatly enhance your hiring potential.

Self Evaluation

When asked what was most difficult for man, Diogenes answered "To know one's self."

When conducting a survey of employers across the country, I asked the question "What advice would you give new college graduates on the threshold of seeking a job?" The most frequent responses fell into the "know yourself" category. In my experience counseling students through the years, the one consistent problem for many was identifying the jobs that would best suit their interests, strengths and weaknesses, likes and dislikes, and their personality. If you are in this category, don't be surprised; you have plenty of company. This is due in no small measure to our highly structured, complex and overly protective system of education. Throughout our lives we are defined by things like grades, financial status, and academic requirements set by others.

Now is the time when you must shed the cocoon of youth and come to grips with your true self. What do you really want from life? How do you expect to achieve *your* objectives? At no time in your life is this more important than when you are seeking that first job after graduation. Now comes the time when you must ask "What do I have to offer?"

Suddenly, you experience an identity crisis. The question "Who am I?" at once becomes a major question. How do you handle it? You think through the whole process and work out your thoughts. As a suggestion, write down your answers, if that will help. You will slowly discover the bits and pieces that are the true you. It's important that you are objective and honest with yourself.

Setting Priorities

It is crucial in the process to identify things that you really like to do and rank them in order of preference. The process of prioritizing your desires will reveal your value system to a large extent. Your value system should play a major role in your decision making.

Here are some questions that might trigger a few answers for you:

Review your entire education, examining the courses you've taken, books you have read, and papers you have written.

Itemize your work experiences: part time, full time, temporary and volunteer.

Note your hobbies, sports, activities, avocations and geographical preferences.

What are your hopes, wishes and desires in the long run?

Do you have certain activities that you can't pursue all the time nor make into an occupation, but certain jobs or locations could provide you with the opportunity to participate in these hobbies on a part time basis and improve your quality of life?

Do you like to work inside or out of doors?

How important is money to you?

As you daydream, think of Joel Hawes' wonderful quotation: "You will be whatever you resolve to be. Determine to be something in the world and you will be something. 'I cannot' never accomplished anything. 'I can' has wrought wonders."

As you work on this exercise, more ideas, thoughts and concepts will evolve. Avoid dealing in generalities, such as "I want to be successful," "I want to make money," and "I like people." For example, being successful usually comes after you have chosen an occupation and pursued it for several years. Select an academic field of study or occupation you enjoy and are capable of handling. Chances are you will then be successful.

One last word on this subject. Most people underestimate their potential contributions and the possibilities they have to offer. Put time and effort into knowing yourself and you will be surprised at the reservoir of talents and abilities you discover. The secret is to channel these talents and abilities properly.

Developing an Interviewing Strategy

When developing an interviewing strategy, it is important to recognize that an employment interview is a *two-way* discussion, and you should feel on equal footing with the employer. Your responses will be much better if you act on this premise. Being defensive and subordinate will not enhance your bargaining position.

Be Confident

How, then, do you develop a frame of mind that enables you to have the confidence to do this? There are several things to realize:

1. The employer has a need to fill a position in order to make the organization function. The employer is going to considerable lengths to hire someone who can best fill that need and it's to the employer's benefit to hire. Presumably, it will cost the employer money if a good candidate is not hired. Thus, it is imperative for you to recognize that you can help the employer, given the opportunity.

2. You have made a considerable investment already in preparing for employment. For example, you have spent at least 16 years of your life getting an education so that you can be productive as an employee. You have taken specialized courses to help you produce for the employer. You have made a tremendous financial investment in preparing for this employment. That is no small contribution. You are prepared to put all of your education, experience and know-how into the job. Just as the employer will make a significant contribution to your well being, so too, will you be contributing to your employer's success and accomplishments.

3. Remember that the interviewer will do all he or she can to make the job opportunity as attractive as possible should you be the desired candidate for employment. By the same token you must make sure all your positive points are well known so the employer can evaluate you in the best light possible. You must

also collect all the information you can about the employer to help yourself match your qualifications with the needs of the employer and to help yourself make a decision should an offer be extended.

4. Above all, think positively when going into the interview.

As you can now tell, your strategy is to be well prepared. Rest assured the interviewer will thoroughly review your resume and any company materials before this session. If you have thoroughly strategized before the interview, your bargaining position will be enhanced tremendously, and, in turn, your chances of being hired will be increased significantly.

Be Prepared

If you are planning on entering a job interview without a great deal of preparation, you are selling yourself short. There are some who can "wing it" but most of us add to our competitive edge by doing homework before the interview.

The ultimate goal of an effective job campaign is landing a position that matches your likes and interests. The objective of the interview is to provide a mutual understanding between you and the employer which is the main vehicle for the job offer.

Interviews vary depending upon the interviewer and the stage of development in your job campaign. For example, the first interview may be a screening session, so an initial applicant pool of many prospects is screened to a desired few. This is usually accomplished by a member of the employer's personnel department, especially if you are a walk-in candidate. Or this task may be completed at a campus placement office. Sometimes, if you represent a specialized discipline such as accounting or engineering, the initial interview will be conducted by an accountant or engineer.

Usually, the next interview is performed with staff from the employing department, normally at the site of the employer's choosing. This is often referred to as an on-site or plant interview. When you go to an interview, remember the following tips:

1. Always take resumes with you when you have an interview, just in case the person talking with you does not have one. At the plant visitation, you may have several interviews with numerous individuals or groups of employers. Be prepared to take psychological tests during these visits, if the employer resorts to such selection techniques.

2. When preparing for the interview, be sure to check all available materials you can obtain on the employer—the annual report, brochures on the product line, locations of facilities, profitability, organizational structure, etc. If you have an opportunity to know the selection criteria before the interview, and this information is frequently made available by the employer in their advertisements and job descriptions, study them carefully to organize your presentation. If you can talk with some current employees of the organization beforehand, this could also be helpful.

3. Be ready to ask questions (covered more completely in Chapter 2).

4. Be properly groomed. Make sure your clothing is consistent with the general attire of employees working for the organization. Good personal hygiene is an absolute.

5. If you have to present any materials in the interview, be sure they are professionally prepared and presented in an attractive manner.

6. Arrive on time. Allow for possible parking problems. Do not arrive a half hour early—five minutes before interview time is about right. If a restroom is nearby, check your attire and grooming beforehand.

7. If the interview takes place at lunch or dinner, avoid alcoholic beverages and smoking as a general rule.

Remember, the interviewer has probably had a lot of experience interviewing. He or she has probably been trained in interviewing techniques, questions to ask, and factors necessary to make the basic decision: Do we want to further consider or hire this individual?

During this interviewing process, you should be thinking in the same vein as you analyze the employer: Do I want to work for this employer, and do I want to proceed with further interviews should they be necessary? Or, have I decided not to work for this organization?

Thinking about all these points and selected issues in advance is important if you want to be properly prepared for the interview. With such preparation you will also be more confident, more relaxed and better able to present yourself in the best light possible.

Be Smart

A great deal of effort goes into the job hunt—preparing the resume, networking, researching, letter writing—but nothing is as important as the interview. This is where the decision is made to hire you. Many people put considerable energy into the job search factors mentioned above but not enough thought and effort into the interview itself.

You can improve your interviewing skills with practice and by using some common sense "smarts." There are a few key points to remember:

1. Relax. Avoid last minute rushes. Advance preparation breeds confidence. After having a few interviews, you will soon feel more at ease and confident.

2. Be yourself. Trying to put on a false face during the interview won't work. You will also feel more comfortable answering questions when you are honest and sincere in your responses. To have a "canned" response to certain questions can only backfire in the long run.

3. Market yourself. All of your responses should relate your qualifications to the job available. Fifty percent of the conversation should be yours. Do not be reluctant to initiate subjects that will enhance your chances.

4. Prepare for the interview by knowing what your responses will be to certain questions. Also, identify questions you will want to ask. Build a bridge between the job and you.

5. Avoid controversial subjects. Don't belabor a cause in which you may have an interest if it doesn't fit into the flow of the interview.

6. Be sure all of your good qualities are known before you end the interview. Some interviewers miss important qualifications in a candidate and it behooves you to make sure that doesn't happen. Have your accomplishments firmly in mind before the interview so you can relate them to the job.

7. Don't speak negatively about your peers, former employers, faculty or other employers. Keep an upbeat and positive approach to all you say in the interview.

8. End the interview with a course of action. Make sure you have closure. This can be when next the interviewer will contact you, when the interviewer will arrange an on-site visit, even rejection. Also, be sure you know what your next step is and when you are to take a certain course of action. In short, summarize what you and the interviewer have decided.

9. Send a thank you letter to the person(s) who interviewed you.

Group Interviews Group interviews can be intimidating to the fresh college graduate but they need not be. A few things to keep in mind are:

1. Take your time in responding to questions.

2. Be sure to talk to all of the people interviewing you. Do not focus on one person and ignore the others.

3. Envision the group interview as a one-on-one interview and don't be reluctant to ask questions and give opinions.

4. Occasionally, there will be one interviewer in the group who is trying to impress the other interviewers rather than ask

prudent questions. Some may be trick questions. Don't let this ruffle you. Take your time and answer in a polite way and by all means avoid being hostile.

Be Careful

The results of an interview are predicated on more than an exchange of words. For example, what you say is important, but how you say it can be equally important. Do you show enthusiasm, energy and interest? These can be shown in *how* you respond to a question as well as what your words are. Your attire, grooming, cleanliness, body language, posture, walk, handshake, eye-to-eye contact, choice of words, speech characteristics, breath, cooperativeness, courtesies you extend, *ad infinitum*—all go into the hopper before you land a job.

Interviewers not only seek to hire people; they also screen out candidates. Exclusive of all your skills, education and experience, negative factors that will screen you out of a job are:

1. Poor appearance

2. Poor attitude

3. Indications of dishonesty

4. Bad-mouthing others

5. Lack of enthusiasm

6. Tardiness

7. Excessive aggressiveness

8. Suspected instability

9. Body odor

10. Questionable eating or drinking habits

11. Indications of lack of dependability

12. Indecisiveness

Do all recruiters put the same value on these factors? No, it varies with the person. You can reduce the wash-out risk by avoiding the above during the interview. Many interviewers put more emphasis on screening *out* candidates than screening *in*, so avoid those factors likely to eliminate you—and thereby enhance your chances of getting hired.

There is a Job for You

The economy plays a major role in the employment of college graduates. The recession of the early 1990s delayed the employment of many seniors entering the world of work. There was no question that many did not have jobs at graduation, though within six months after graduation most of them found employment. Certainly those who continued to work hard at finding employment were eventually successful. Many employers cut staff during this period, mainly experienced personnel. This creates a bubble in the manpower pipeline and eventually vacancies created will be filled by graduating seniors.

In 1991, in a survey of employers by the Collegiate Employment Research Institute, the majority replied that they did not think there was a shortage of college graduates. Certain employer categories thought there was a surplus, in some areas, including automotive and mechanical equipment companies, electronic and electrical equipment manufacturers, aerospace and its components, and banking, finance and insurance industries. These fluctuations receive considerable media attention, but don't conclude there are no jobs. When interviewing it is important to remember that you are one person looking for one job. There is always one good job out there for you. Never give up on looking for the job you want—regardless of the economy, what the media say, or the number of rejection slips you gather.

Even if the first position you accept is not all you expected it to be you always have the option of changing. Turnover for technical graduates averages about 5 percent in the first year and non-technical graduates are about double that. Over a three-year period turnover averages about 20 percent for technical and 30 percent for nontechnical personnel.

Industries vary greatly in turnover, with aerospace leading. Others with higher than average turnover on the nontechnical side are the hospitality, communications, hospital and retailing industries. Turnover varies greatly by industry, employer and economic conditions, however, and you must judge each organization on its individual characteristics.

Recruiters...What You Can Expect

You can expect to encounter a wide range of recruiters. Most campus recruiters are full time employees of the employing organization, but not necessarily full time in recruiting. Depending upon your major you may be interviewed by personnel department staff or by specialists from the various units within an organization, i.e., engineering, accounting, marketing.

Age, skill, personality and experience vary greatly. Expect all kinds of interviewers and interviews. Neither will follow a standard pattern. There may be cases where the student has to carry the interview to keep the discussion on a track that brings out the best in a candidate, though most of the time the recruiter will lead the interview. The personality of the recruiter is often the personality of the employer, but not always. Do not predicate your further interest in a company on the campus recruiter. On the other hand, you can be fairly certain your on-site interviews will be representative of the personality of the employer.

Some recruiters will have a narrow understanding of the total personnel needs of the organization. This is often the case when recruiters represent only certain departments or functions of the company. Most recruiters, if not knowledgeable about the needs in the company for a person with your discipline, will refer your resume to the appropriate departments for perusal. Usually, the larger employers have a campus representative who can speak to all the personnel needs.

Generally speaking, campus recruiters are skilled at interviewing. While they don't always make the final decision as to who is hired, and where, they play a prominent role in referring and recommending candidates. Never underestimate their importance to your being hired.

Getting the Right Interview

For those students at schools where excellent placement programs exist, the student should take advantage of all the opportunity afforded by those services. On many campuses this can be a primary source of interviews for most students.

Career Planning and Placement Offices

When using the career planning and placement office, take advantage of the full range of interviewing possibilities. First off, learn the system. Too often students do not take the time to learn about the many employers who seek applicants from their schools. The students were "too busy" to review bulletins on employers interviewing on campus and the jobs they were attempting to fill. The senior year is a busy time for most graduates; it is nevertheless necessary to take the time to talk to the employers when they are visiting on campus. This process is much more efficient than most other recruitment methods. It also provides an opportunity to have face-to-face contact with employers who might not otherwise be available to you for interviews.

Take advantage of the career library to learn more about employers. Visit with career advisors, as they may hear of leads not listed in placement bulletins for employers visiting campus. Attend career fairs so you can personally talk with employers. Any time you can make contact with employers on an individual basis is always better than approaches by telephone or letter.

Finally, be sure your credentials are on file at the placement office at all times during your senior year. Employers periodically contact placement offices for credentials of graduating students, prior to campus visit or to fill immediate openings. Review bulletins and other information on employment opportunities distributed by your college placement office.

The Hidden Job Market

Contrary to what many people believe, most entry level jobs for graduating seniors are not filled by interviews with recruiting representatives on campus. A recent study indicated that of those employers *visiting campuses*, 42 percent of those hired were hired through this process in their companies. They hire about 12 percent by write-in resumes and applications. Don't be misled by these statistics, however, because most employers do not visit campuses to recruit for various reasons—too small, not enough demand, too costly, etc.

Thus, the graduating senior must not ignore the Hidden Job Market that literally is all around. This applies in good times and bad, winter and summer, all over the country.

Advertised and posted jobs, especially for government jobs, constitute a large portion of the positions available, but there are still many other options.

Exploiting the hidden job market takes creativity, innovation and a special kind of initiative to generate the many opportunities available through this method. Here are a few:

Personal contacts.   Probably more people find jobs from personal contacts than through any other method. Do not be reluctant to let people know you are looking for a job. Their contacts include friends, family relations, neighbors, faculty members, college alumni, and business associates of the aforementioned individuals. Attending conferences and professional meetings can also be an excellent source of leads. This is a form of networking to inform people that you are looking for employment and/or to ask advice on whom they would recommend you talk to about setting up an interview. This is also referred to as "pyramiding"—contacts with one individual to gain an interview with another.

Help wanted advertisements. These provide another source of job opportunities. National newspapers such as the *New York Times,* the *Wall Street Journal,* the *Los Angeles Times* and the *Chicago Tribune* are excellent sources and can provide many leads. If you have a geographic preference for Denver, for instance, you could subscribe to a Denver newspaper. Using this method can help you zero in on a particular area. Blind advertisements, without the employer's name mentioned, contrary to some people's opinion, can lead to good opportunities. Some are recruitment efforts for lower level commission sales positions or related assignments.

Membership lists. Such helpful references from associations are another source of leads to contact (see appendix). One of the best is the *College Placement Annual,* which lists most major employers seeking college graduates throughout the nation. Other journals, professional magazines, and directories can provide a vast number of leads.

Employment agencies. Sometimes helpful, but experience suggests that they are not the best source of job opportunities for most seniors—other than in the highly technical fields.

"Contract" employers. Increasingly popular, such employers have provided satisfactory job options for some graduates. When hired by a contract employer, you are hired by one company at their salary and benefit program and they then sell your services to another company.

Contacts made through summer employment, internships and part time employment. All are excellent leads for getting the right interviews. In fact, many employers use these precedents to recruit many of their permanent employees.

Professional organizations. Almost all associations often offer placement services to their members. Many also sponsor career fairs, job campaigning seminars, and career conferences.

Federal and state government job lists. The Civil Services regularly list their job openings. Be prepared for a slower employment process when applying to government agencies versus business or industry. Many excellent career opportunities are available to new college graduates interested in government employment.

The United State Employment Services (U.S.E.S.). This has not been a highly productive source for most graduating college students, but sometimes seniors get jobs through these services.

You must be a self-starter to get the right interviews. Determination and aggressiveness are required. You must be prepared for negative responses—but not let those responses get you down. It only takes one "yes" and you are on your way! This is one area where persistence pays off. Identify the right targets and your chances of hitting the bullseye are greatly enhanced. And remember, the more contacts you make the greater your chances for success. Finally, remember that arranging interviews takes time, effort, and money to do it properly. Prepare yourself mentally and financially—and schedule the time necessary to do it properly.

Computer Databases

Another very good source of interviewing opportunities is computer databases. Depending upon the techniques used and the costs of these databases, their potential can be rated from very good to poor. This is a fairly recent innovation using personal computers to bring candidates and employers together.

Computerized resume services. The computerized resume service is one direct marketing option sold by numerous head hunters. The process of registering for one of these services is very easy. Each applicant completes a resume profile including career interests, prior work experiences, academic achievements, salary requirements, special skills and abilities, and geographical preferences. Interested employers search the database using the job description for each available employment opportunity. By refining the selection criteria, employers can reduce the available applicants to a limited number for interviews.

Most in demand by prospective employers using these databases are any applicants in high visibility academic majors, high tech fields, women applicants in predominately male-dominated occupations, and minority applicants in almost any demanded job category. For an applicant pool containing several of these applicants, employers will pay very well.

This recruiting method is used as merely one source in a total recruitment program. Most employers still visit college campuses for conducting interviews, rely on current employees for referrals, and sometimes resort to printed advertisements to encourage more applicants.

The primary costs for these databases are paid by the prospective employers. These fees will vary from $50 to $100 per search, or $1,500 to $3,000 for unlimited searches during a year. To be listed in one of these databases is normally free or inexpensive for new college graduates, usually costing from $10 to $50 for two months, six months, or a year. Experienced candidates or those seeking higher starting salaries may have to pay a slightly higher fee.

Also note, however, that some employers measure worth of resumes in these databases using the following criteria: grade point averages, prior career related work experiences, campus leadership positions attained, and degrees received. If your academic record and prior work experiences are marginal, your probability of being selected from one of these databases is not very good.

Examples. Several examples of these databases include kiNexus, Resume-Link, the Restrac Resume Reader, Jobhunt, the College Recruitment Database, ABRATRAK Applicant Tracking System, AMA-Applicant Management System, ATS-Applicant Tracking System, ATS-III, Jet*Scan national databank, CompuSource, and Ross Data Services. More are arriving in college placement offices each month. Other systems were discontinued because of financing problems, technical difficulties, or lack of national acceptance. It might be a good idea to inquire into the financial solvency of these resume services before paying any fees.

Computerized job listings. Job listings are accumulated in databases as another technique marketed by computer vendors. As one example, the National Employment Wire Service (NEWS) database collects employment opportunities from local newspapers and distributes this information via computer modem to college placement offices. By using this source, prospective employers can be identified from numerous regions around the country, but keep in mind that you must send the employers a resume and cover letter, and then visit these prospective employers in person, possibly at your own expense, before you can be hired. So, do not become too enthusiastic about sending resumes to every matching job listing. Someone must pay for this trip to visit the employer—and it could be you.

Examples. Besides the NEWS system, other examples include the Career Advisory Network, Peterson's Connexion system, Datext business databases, and DIALOG databases. Before entering any of these databases, review their success history. Ask questions about the numbers of individuals hired previously from each. Learn about the employers utilizing each source and the academic majors pursued by these employers. Also make yourself aware of the costs involved—to you and the prospective employer, and any potential commissions on your starting salary.

Although these databases can be quite helpful for identifying potential employers, the tasks of interviewing with the employer and landing the job are still your responsibility.

Computerized placement office systems. Contact your college or university placement office to determine their automation capabilities. Some placement offices register graduating students and alumni via computer terminals, and referrals from these databases often yield additional interviewing opportunities. It is also possible to access these databases with your own personal computer. Register with them when appropriate, and use them to identify job prospects related to your background and preferences.

This area of cultivating contacts is really in the developmental stages and has to be refined to be totally efficient. It is a source of contacts, however, and can be helpful to certain candidates in selected disciplines.

Generating Interviews through Mass Mailings

For most graduating seniors, blind mass mailing of resumes to employers is not very efficient unless you have special skills and have an exceptional educational and experience background. Where the supply/demand ratio heavily favors the candidate, doors can be opened via this method, but even then, persons with the outstanding and exceptional characteristics would do better to more precisely target their prospective employers. A survey made a few years ago showed that of employers visiting campuses, about 10 percent of the total graduates hired were "write-ins."

Many college recruiters hire very few people via submitted resumes. It simply is not an efficient way to recruit. Large corporations receive tens of thousands of resumes in the mail each year; one organization received over 300,000 resumes through the mail, unrequested. While any staff would like to spend more time reviewing resumes, most of the paper will be reviewed for not more than five to twenty seconds. That means thousands of hours of valuable time has been wasted when that time could have been spent much more productively.

Also, mass mailings work better with smaller employers than larger ones, simply because of the difference in volume received by each. Small, entrepreneurial employers are apt to be more receptive to the inquiring candidate than those in the Fortune 500 ranks.

Marketing Yourself

Excellent marketing skills really make a difference when interviewing with prospective employers, and you can develop those talents much more than you might think with a little planning and some effort on your part.

One of the first superficial liabilities for most first-job-seekers is a lack of experience. Yet, college students have far more experience than they realize. For instance, you have energy, experience dealing with people, part time and summer work experiences. Regardless of the menial labor required by the job, you understand the value of work and the techniques required to work well with others. Identify the skills you have learned from athletics, club memberships, travel and hobbies. Relate to the job you are seeking your college course work, papers you have written, and the experiences you have gained from 16 or more years of education. Try to avoid developing an inferiority complex about your lack of experience. There are thousands of jobs on the employment market that can use a person with the above-mentioned experience.

There are numerous statistical ratios that could be helpful when developing your marketing strategy. There are proven methods for generating sales of products and services. You can use the same strategies when selling yourself. The following chart demonstrates one example:

Developing leads of 100

Generates 25 possible prospective employers

Leading to 15 definite prospects

Generating 10 interviews

Yielding two offers

Resulting in one job acceptance

This method of marketing your talents demonstrates that you

must be able to accept rejection and move on. As you proceed, minimize your weaknesses and maximize your strengths. Talent is always important in any job-seeking effort, but recognize that it is not always talent alone that lands the job. Talent plus timing is often the combination that breeds success.

Your Own Marketing Plan

At the foundation of successfully marketing your skills is your marketing plan. First you must prioritize your interests, likes, dislikes, goals and abilities so you have a well defined career objective. Then schedule your interviews with those employers whom you think can best help you reach your objective. Contacts can be generated from friends, lists, directories, placement offices, libraries and professional organizations.

Then prepare for the interviews as covered in "Developing an Interviewing Strategy" earlier in this chapter. Achieve a positive attitude toward your recruiter and the interview outcome. It helps if you remember that every rejection brings you closer to acceptance since there is a definite ratio between the number of rejections and the final acceptance. While this ratio varies for each individual and the employers involved, sooner or later the acceptance factor emerges.

Appearance, also mentioned earlier, is a critical factor when marketing yourself. Many interviewers make their decisions regarding future consideration for employment within the first five to ten minutes of an interview. In fact, your appearance conveys a message about you that words cannot convey. Appearance becomes especially important in initial interviews since it opens the doors for further interviews and more detailed analysis of your credentials.

Dress is an extremely important part of your overall appearance, so do not be reluctant to spend a few dollars on your clothing and accessories. Emphasize quality. Most students have limited financial resources in their senior years, but here is one place where a small investment can make a major difference.

Some basics to remember:

1. Pay attention to your grooming, (i.e., clean fingernails and proper hair care).

2. For most business jobs, wear conservative, classic clothing in darker tones. Medium blues, navy and gray are best bets for men; blues, black, dark brown and burgundy are good choices for women.

3. For men, suits are best, although when finances won't allow it, a well-pressed sports coat with proper matching pants is acceptable. Most employers recognize that recent college graduates are not loaded with money, but they do expect you to be neat and clean. For women, classic suits are always acceptable; dresses are very good, providing an opportunity for a little more creativity. Avoid extremes in skirt lengths and bright colors. Sweaters and skirts are marginal at best.

4. Shoes make a difference. Be sure your shoes are shined. Leather is best. For men, brogues do well and loafers are acceptable with black or brown recognized as the best colors. For women, classic pumps are always proper with a 1 1/2–2 inch heel. Black, navy, and brown are the best colors.

Another fundamental of a good interview is to place yourself mentally on equal footing with the interviewer. Don't feel inferior or that the interviewer holds all the cards. Obviously, don't be too aggressive and kill your job chances immediately. But do sit upright in your chair and speak clearly.

Generally speaking, the interviewer and the candidate should each speak about 50 percent of the time during the interview, although this varies. Make sure your best points are known to the interviewer and all your questions are answered before terminating the interview. Keep your liabilities to yourself. Avoid negative comments about former employers, faculty or your college. When appropriate, use positive statements about past employers or faculty.

Listen carefully to the interviewer. Concentrate on the questions asked and think before you provide answers, especially when replying to open-ended questions. And do not be reluctant to ask questions. Remember, a good interview is a two-way street.

Be sure your best strengths are mentioned but keep your weaknesses to yourself unless specifically encouraged to comment on them. Then be truthful. If questions are asked regarding your use of drugs, answer honestly. Most larger companies require physical examinations that include drug testing.

In spite of all of the cautions mentioned above, it is important that you be yourself. Trying to be someone that you are not has numerous pitfalls.

Finally, follow-up after the interview is another chance to market yourself. A good follow-up letter reminds the interviewer of your visit and reinforces your quest for the job. Often he or she will be interviewing many candidates, and sometimes individual candidates tend to blur in the interviewer's mind. If your follow-up letter doesn't bring a response in ten days to two weeks, follow up with a telephone call to reinforce your interest in the position.

The Resume as It Relates to the Interview

The resume is an important tool when preparing for the job interview. This document conveys all your experiences, academic preparation, and relevant information pertaining to your qualifications. It makes you think about your prior accomplishments, your methods of achievement, and your future career prospects. Properly prepared, it gives you an outline to assist you immensely in the interviewing process.

In fact, the greatest value received by anyone who prepares a resume may come from the review it gives you before the interview. It helps you place in chronological order your activities, restoring experiences that you might not consider prior to an interview without having prepared a resume. Depending upon the type of resume you prepare, in addition to placing your facts in chronological order, it will help you recreate your experiences, provide reasons for selecting your career paths, identify your achievements, and fit your skills and abilities with the employer's needs.

Having prepared your resume, you are provided with a database from which to draw your answers to questions during the interview. The resume refreshes your memory. The resume also can be the focal point for the interview, depending upon the employer's style of interviewing. In most cases, it complements the interviewing process. Obviously, great care and effort should be taken to assure that the combination of the resume and the interview present you in the best possible way.

A poorly prepared resume—poor punctuation, misspelled words, incorrect grammar—can obviously eliminate the possibility of an interview. Should you get an interview in spite of a poorly prepared resume, it could start you off on the wrong foot with a prospective employer. As image-making tool, the resume should be in concert with the professionalism of the interview. Having a strong resume can make the difference in your selection for a position. Treat it as one of the most significant documents in your job campaign.

There are many uses for a resume other than providing a picture of your background. For example, preparing a resume helps you organize your education, experiences, and objectives when seeking career alternatives. It can be given to references so they can respond better to inquiries about you. Faculty or summer employers may not always know as much about you as you think.

A resume should be left with individuals whom you contact when networking. It can open doors that you can't reach through personal contacts. A resume can project your qualifications in a positive manner. It can serve as the basis for an interview. It can be helpful when completing employer application forms, and may become part of your permanent record with an employer.

When preparing a resume, be brief. Chances are, initially it will be scanned quickly. Use action words that succinctly tell your story. Appearance of the resume is important. Good quality, off white or beige paper is a safe bet. Usually one page is sufficient, although two pages are acceptable. Do not crowd the margins, and, of course, make sure the spelling and grammar are proper. Layout is important for emphasis and overall appearance.

Negotiating as Part of the Interviewing Process

Whenever you enter a negotiating situation, it is important that you determine and maintain firm objectives. Career opportunity should be foremost in your thinking. Be realistic in your bargaining position and be honest when evaluating your market value.

At the same time, be optimistic about your career goals. There is usually some give and take before final agreement is reached. On those items fixed in your mind as extremely important and not negotiable, do not compromise. Minimum salary required to exist might be an example. Keep in mind, however, that you are just getting started in a career and opportunity is more important than starting salary.

Before going into an interview, try to understand the employer's bargaining position and their general criteria for hiring personnel. Knowing the employer's alternatives can make a major difference in your expectations.

Be sure to cover all the basics when negotiating—starting salary, benefits, expected travel, starting date, moving expenses, holidays, housing, training. Avoid getting into highly specific discussions of these items until it appears that the employer is interested in hiring you. You will never be in a better position to negotiate than at this point.

When the employer makes a job offer, there is a desire among many to accept the offer on the spot. Absolutely avoid this temptation! Be sure you understand the offer. Ideally, try to get the offer in writing, including all the details.

After getting an offer, if it doesn't meet your expectations, then you may want to shift your requirements to sometime in the future. For example, if the starting salary offer doesn't meet your expectations, ask if a raise is possible within three or six months, assuming your work is acceptable. Again, get this part of the agreement in writing. You may want to accept a negotiated offer on the telephone but be sure it is confirmed in writing.

Recent graduates having numerous interviews often receive several offers. Before accepting an offer, complete all your scheduled interviews, even though most employers will not wait more than a few weeks before withdrawing a job offer. However, if you have a legitimate reason for an extension, be sure to discuss it with the employer. After reviewing all your potential opportunities, accept the most attractive option.

Do not renege on an acceptance once you have made a deal. Nor should an employer renege on an offer and acceptance. The College Placement Council has established a Code of Ethics recommended for employers and graduates that is fair and equitable. This code is available in most placement offices; read it before interviewing.

Check List for Fringe Benefits

Fringe benefits are an important part of the compensation package. Some counselors advise not to worry about fringe benefits, especially when you are first starting out on a career. Wrong! Benefits can be a substantial part of what you receive for your work, running as high as 30 to 35 percent of your salary, depending upon the employer. Not all employers offer the same benefits. Some pay the cost of all benefits; more often the benefit costs are shared between employer and employee.

Here are some of the common employee benefits offered by many employers and the percentage of companies offering each type:

Common employee benefits offered

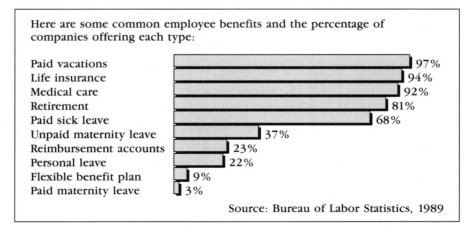

Here are some common employee benefits and the percentage of companies offering each type:

Benefit	Percentage
Paid vacations	97%
Life insurance	94%
Medical care	92%
Retirement	81%
Paid sick leave	68%
Unpaid maternity leave	37%
Reimbursement accounts	23%
Personal leave	22%
Flexible benefit plan	9%
Paid maternity leave	3%

Source: Bureau of Labor Statistics, 1989

Following is a list of benefits and who pays for those benefits:

Benefit	**Who Pays**
1. Retirement benefits.	Usually employer.
2. Life insurance.	Usually employer. Employee may pay supplemental costs.
3. Medical insurance.	Costs usually shared between employer and employee. Look into option carefully so that your particular needs are met.
4. Vacation.	Usually two weeks/year for 1st 3 to 5 years. Three weeks after 3 to 15 years. Four weeks after 15 years.
5. Holidays	Employer paid. Usually 8 to 10 days per year.
6. Sick leave.	Varies greatly with company.
7. Dental insurance.	Costs usually shared. Not always offered by employer.
8. Disability insurance.	Costs usually shared. Not always offered by employer.
9. Tuition assistance	Most large companies pay all or part of tuition, books, etc. Usually employer only pays for courses related to work.
10. Child care.	Cost usually shared, but not all employers provide child care though some do.

11. Bonuses.

Cash awards based on performance or suggestions.

12. Commission.

Cash awards based on volume of sales. Remuneration can be 100% of sales or combination of salary and commission.

13. Draw.

Weekly or monthly amount paid regularly against commission sales.

14. Stock purchase.

Employers offer employee stock at price below market value.

15. Matching Saving Plan.

Employers match employees' savings up to a certain percentage of salary.

Work Schedules

"The old order changeth making way for the new." This adage is particularly applicable to the work schedules recently (mainly since the early 1980s) adopted by many employers. The 36 to 40 hour work week is still the standard for most employers, but this is rapidly being shortened, lengthened, compressed and sliced into many different formats.

Following are some of the work schedules enjoyed by some employees. These plans vary greatly among employers and even departments within companies.

Compressed work week. By adjusting the hours per day worked, employees work 40 hours per week in 4 days (10 hours per day) and eliminate one work day.

Part time work day.   Employees work one quarter, one half or three quarter time and are paid accordingly. Some employers offer benefit packages to these employees on a pro-rata basis. Others do not.

Flex time.   Hours are arranged by mutual consent of employer and employee. This alternative cannot be arranged in many organizations because of the nature of the work. With those employees with whom it is possible, it is becoming popular. Can be ideal for working mothers.

Shared jobs.   Usually two people work half time each to fill a full time job. Requires good cooperation between employees. Ideal for working mothers.

Temporary work.   Very popular with most employers. Allows employer to meet peek demand periods of production. Benefits limited if for shorter than 6 month periods.

Home-based work.   Work is performed at home. Ideal for jobs such as editing, telephone sales, direct sales.

Overtime.   Employer usually pays time and a half for overtime over 40 hours. Many salaried positions graduating seniors would fill require more than 40 hours per week for which there is no additional pay over 40 hours. Job candidates are advised to find out during the interview what the expectations are with regard to pay for overtime.

Salary Negotiations

Doing your homework on your marketability and the employer's salary policies can pay handsome dividends. Research the average salaries for people with your experience and education. Such information can usually be found in the career planning center, the placement office, the College Placement Council Salary Survey, and other published surveys. Not all college graduates start at the same salary. In fact, some majors start, on average, at twice the salary of other majors. Graduates of some of the better known schools sometimes command higher salaries than graduates from lesser known schools. Employers in the same business have a wide range in their salary schedules. Certain industries traditionally pay more than others. By doing your homework you should have a fairly good idea of the salary you should receive from a given employer.

When negotiating remuneration, be sure to include all the factors—salary, vacation time, bonuses, medical benefits, employer paid benefits and employee paid cost for benefits, expenses, transportation and education allowances, relocation expenses, salary review periods, dental and optical insurance coverage, and other forms of remuneration.

Timing and having all the facts in hand so you understand your bargaining position are important. Leave the discussion on salary to the interviewer unless it's not brought up—in which case you gracefully broach the subject. Some employers advertise their salary ranges to candidates, in which you know in advance the general parameters. Still, there often is room for negotiation and employers do bargain, depending upon their bargaining position and company restraints. Remember, though, that once on the job your potential for negotiating further salary adjustments is reduced considerably and your bargaining position has eroded.

Timing

Regardless of the endeavor you are pursuing in the world of work, timing is important. Thus it is with interviewing and finding success in the job market.

For a new graduate just finishing college, control over timing is difficult. For example, a person graduating at a time when there are massive layoffs in business and government will experience limited job opportunities. Others who graduate when the economy is booming and employers are on a hiring binge will find excellent job opportunities. Few college graduates have much control over the date of their graduation.

Recognize a difficult job market situation when you face it and realize that you must work harder to generate interviews. Prepare for more rejection letters and seriously consider the possibility that you may have to settle for something less than what you expected. When anticipating a tight labor market, you will want to start interviewing early in your senior year and certainly not less than six months before you expect to begin working.

When the economy is healthy, be sure to complete all your interviews with the desired employers, since you may receive several offers. You will want to be sure to settle on the best one. Being alert to the job market will give you the sense of aggressiveness needed for landing a good job offer.

chapter two

Preparing for the Interview

Normally, 50 percent of an interview will consist of questions about you and your background, experiences, interests, likes and dislikes, motivations, attitudes, skills and abilities. You must be prepared to answer numerous questions centering on these points. To best answer these questions you must know yourself—and to know one's self is one of the most difficult problems any person faces in day-to-day living.

Questions, Questions

If you feel you don't know your wants in a career, start the process by asking yourself some basic questions. For example:

1. What would I like to do?

2. What motivates me?

3. What am I prepared to do?

4. If asked, "What is your objective in this interview?" how would I answer the question?

5. How important is money to me?

6. Where would I most like to live?

7. Which employers would make my career most enjoyable?

8. Do I plan to obtain additional education?

9. When can I begin working?

10. What are my assets and liabilities?

11. Why do I want this job?

Start with these questions of yourself, and add as many other questions as you can think of. Take time, write your answers. This process will help you get a clearer picture of yourself and will definitely help you during the interview. You will come across as knowing yourself and your objectives. Contrast this with the person who flounders on some answers to these questions; that interview isn't nearly as successful.

Students are often confused when having to answer real life questions after being exposed to a multitude of philosophies, lifestyles, and opinions while attending college. Crystallizing all this input in advance will help you know yourself, and in turn this will enhance your outcome for a successful interview.

Some Sample Questions

Prepare yourself for all kinds of questions in an interview, since recruiters have a wide range of questions to ask when interviewing graduating seniors. Robert Greenberg and Billy Craig of the Career Planning and Placement Office at the University of Tennessee at Knoxville surveyed students' reactions to employer interviewing questions. Here are some of the questions, for better or worse, that the students reported:

Best questions:

Tell me about yourself.

What are your strengths and weaknesses?

What did you learn in your last job?

What would you consider an ideal job?

Describe a pressure situation you've experienced and how you handled it.

Why did you choose your major?

Why should we hire you?

Worst questions:

Tell me about yourself.

How would a friend describe you?

What are your strengths and weaknesses?

What does your father do for a living?

Are you dating anyone regularly?

Have you ever been arrested or fired?

Most difficult questions:

Tell me about yourself.

Expand on your resume.

What are your greatest weaknesses?

What do your friends dislike about you?

What is the toughest decision you've had to make?

What can you do for our company?

Questions You Should Be Prepared to Answer

Each interview is a unique experience and the range of differences among interviews is infinite. Personalities, chemistry between people, type of organization, time differences, interview types (campus, on-site, etc.), technical compared to nontechnical interviews, interview setting, nature of job, qualification emphasis of the job opening, and experience of interviewer are just some of the factors that make each interview different from any other.

Nevertheless, employment interviews generally have much in common. Knowing this, you should be aware that proper preparation can enhance your chances for landing the job. Provided below is a partial list of questions you should be prepared to answer, even though you may not experience all of these questions in any one given interview. Rehearsing these questions in advance can make your answers more explicit and should add to your confidence during the interview.

Your answers should always convey professionalism, accomplishment, honesty, diligence, and grace under pressure. Whenever possible, highlight your productivity and efficiency. *How* you answer questions can make a big difference in your success.

In this context, then, here are some of the questions and comments you should be prepared to answer:

1. Tell me about yourself.

2. Why are you interested in this position?

3. Why should we hire you?

4. What do you consider your strengths and weaknesses?

5. Why did you select this university for your academic preparation?

6. Why did you choose to major in _____ ?

7. How were your college expenses financed?

8. What is your overall grade point average?

9. What is the grade point average in your major?

10. Do you have any geographical restrictions?

11. What goals have you established for yourself?

12. What do you do in your spare time?

13. What are your salary expectations?

14. Have you ever used drugs?

15. Do you have any physical disabilities that would impair your employment with us?

16. How did you like your last employer?

17. Where do you expect to be in five or ten years?

18. What do you know about our organization?

19. Tell me about the lessons learned in your internship, summer employment, co-op experience, etc.

20. What position in our organization interests you?

21. Are you willing to travel?

22. Have you changed your major while in college?

23. What qualifications do you have that would make you particularly qualified for this job?

24. How did you happen to apply for this job?

25. Do you feel you have attained the best scholastic record of which you are capable?

26. Tell me about your experience in the armed services (if applicable).

27. What are your plans for graduate school (if any)?

28. When could you make a visit to our plant site for further interviews?

29. When are you available for employment?

30. Have I missed anything?

31. If I called your former supervisor and requested an evaluation of your work, what would he/she tell me?

There will be other specific questions, obviously, pertaining to your resume, education and work experiences.

Questions You Should be Prepared to Ask

Remember that an interview is a two-way street. You must look at the interview as an opportunity for the employer to gain information about you, but you must also receive information about the job and the employer. This is a very important point, but many graduating seniors fail to get all the information they need to make proper decisions during their job searches.

If your placement office provides workshops on interviewing techniques, attend them, especially if you have limited experience with the interviewing process. Make a list of any questions you want employers to answer *before* going into the interview. Memorize them. Make sure you ask these questions before leaving the interview.

Time is also important when asking questions. For example, avoid asking questions on benefits or salary in the initial phases of the interview. Be aware of the approximate length of the interview, so you can get all your questions answered before the interview time has ended. This is especially true at the on-campus interview, since these sessions are usually 20 to 30 minutes long and a rigid time schedule is maintained. By all means, make sure your best points are known before you leave the interview. The interviewer will not always emphasize these points, so it behooves you to assume that responsibility. Obviously, different positions elicit different questions, but the following list includes some general questions you should be prepared to ask:

1. Who was the last person to hold this job, and what is he or she doing now?

2. Who will be my immediate supervisor? You should request an opportunity to meet this person during an on-site visit.

3. What are the possibilities for promotion?

4. What is the organizational structure, and where does this position fit in?

5. What is the extent of travel required on this job?

6. What are housing conditions in the surrounding geographical area?

7. What is the starting salary for this position?

8. What is the current financial condition of the organization?

9. Specifically, what will my duties be (if not already discussed)?

10. Do you have a training program for this position? If so, please briefly explain the program.

11. Are graduate degree programs available to employees in this position?

12. I am interested in this position. When will I hear from you regarding further action on my application?

Time is of the essence for a successful job search. Seniors find it very easy to delay and not devote enough time to their job hunting efforts. It's not too early to start planning your job search when you return to college in the fall of your senior year. Take an inventory of everything it will take to carry out your job campaign. Identify the procedures you intend to follow when carrying out your objectives. For example, the best avenues to pursue for getting job leads; the placement office operations; employer lists; personal contacts and networking; references; completing credentials; scheduling time for interviews; seeking faculty and other contacts' advice; attending workshops; planning a self-marketing strategy; attending professional conferences; and studying the competition and the job market at large.

By completing your homework in advance, you can prepare to enter a full-blown job search about five to six months before you graduate. You will also avoid the last minute stress of many college graduates by having a well-organized plan in mind.

Things to Do Before an Interview

Research Prospective Employers

You know how you feel when an employer knows about you and your background; you feel flattered when they show a special interest in you. The same is true for an employer. By knowing a company's products, financial condition, job opportunities, growth pattern and organization, you are reflecting a special interest and enthusiasm for the employer. An absence of this knowledge can reflect negatively on your application, especially if your competition has done homework.

Once you have this information be sure to relate it to your interests, background and experience, and be sure to let the employer know there is a good match between their needs and your qualifications.

Sources for researching employers can be found in your career information center or library. Company profiles are available in *College Placement Annual* or *Peterson's Annual* guides. *Dun and Bradstreet* and *Standard and Poor's* also have much helpful information on various organizations. Check your local reference librarian for a wealth of information in the areas that interest you.

Researching an employer can play a substantial role in making an interview successful. This knowledge will provide you with the opportunity to speak intelligently to the recruiter. Furthermore, this knowledge can tell you if this is an organization you *don't* want as your new employer.

Plenty of effort is necessary to properly complete this task, but all the effort is well worth it, since the prospective employer is duly impressed with your presentation, and you are very familiar with the situation you face with this prospective employer.

Here are some questions to ask yourself in order to decide if a company is really for you:

1. What does this job involve?

2. Does the culture of the employer fit my personality?

3. Are these the kind of people with whom I would enjoy working?

4. Will I enjoy the work?

5. Will this job interfere with my family?

6. Is the company financially sound?

7. Is this the geographical area I want?

8. Does the job fit my long-range goals?

9. Do I feel good about accepting the offer?

10. Will I have adequate training?

11. Are the work hours reasonable?

12. Is the commuting distance reasonable?

13. Does my family think this offer is a good one?

14. Is there another place available where I could do better?

15. Is the salary adequate?

Clear References with Faculty and Others

A minor task, but a thoughtful and wise one, is to let people know you would like to use them as a reference. It alerts them to possible calls and affords you the opportunity to brief them about your interest—which can strengthen the reference's response. It is good to send references a copy of your resume so they will be able to speak accurately and knowledgeably about you.

Study Job Descriptions and Relate Your Background to the Job

Always try to get a job description for any job you are seeking. This gives you a target when writing a resume. It also helps you focus during the interview. This information provides you with an opportunity to explain the match of your education, experience, and interests with the employer's position.

Many interviews end with the candidate diluting the thrust of his or her efforts by focusing on a nonexistent vacancy. By knowing the duties and responsibilities of an available job, you can relate more explicitly to the needs of the employer.

Practice Interview Techniques

It is a good idea to practice interviewing with a fellow student or in workshop practice sessions before getting that all-important first job interview. Many students prepare for interviewing by taking interviews with employers who interest them very little or an organization with whom they have little chance of landing a job. After these practice interviews, they can then approach their prime prospects. Having experience with several interviewers helps the novice hone interviewing skills. In fact, many employers feel that graduating students become more capable at their interviewing skills as the recruitment season progresses. Practice makes perfect.

Interviewers vary greatly in their methods, so don't expect a similar format from each one. When practicing, adopt the frame of mind that you are on equal footing with the interviewer. Confidence is important to a successful interview and practice can help you develop that confidence. You will find that interviewers are human, just like you.

When practicing try to be succinct in your responses since, in the campus interview especially, you have limited time to present your case—generally 20 to 30 minutes. Learn to focus on your strengths and articulate those capabilities.

Practice can also help keep you from floundering when confronted with a question pertaining to a liability. Know, for example, how you will handle questions regarding a low grade point average, if that is your situation.

Do's and Don'ts

In addition to being prepared for interview questions coming from any direction, here are a few do's and don'ts for any interviewing situation:

Do:

1. Be on time.

2. Be neat and properly dressed.

3. Bring extra copies of your resume to the interview.

4. Practice interviewing.

5. Study potential questions and your probable answers to them before interviewing.

6. Know your travel and location restrictions, if any.

7. Analyze your strengths and be sure the interviewer is aware of them before completing the interview.

8. Know your overall and your major grade point averages.

9. Know the market for a person with your talents and be realistic in your salary demands.

10. Know your military status.

11. Advise the appropriate people you would like to use them for references.

12. Be prepared to answer questions pertaining to drugs and alcohol.

13. Be positive in your responses.

14. Respect subordinates of the individual conducting the interview.

15. End the interview with an expected course of action.

16. Thank the interviewer.

17. Keep a record of all interviews conducted.

18. Write a follow-up thank you letter.

19. Recognize that you may receive some rejections but do not let this damage your enthusiasm.

20. Consider all potential job leads and do not limit your efforts to placement services interviews (include networking, newspaper advertisements, directories, etc).

21. Be straightforward.

22. Take the initiative if an employer doesn't follow up as agreed to in an interview.

23. Remember that *you* are the one responsible for getting a job—don't rely on others.

24. If you want a drink at lunch or dinner or during a reception with an employer, stay with a light drink.

25. Listen intently.

26. Remember that you can negotiate.

27. Be honest.

28. Be professional.

29. Follow up, on time, with everything you say you will do.

Don't:

1. Be a threat to the interviewer.

2. Be late or too early for your appointment.

3. Dwell on your liabilities.

4. Discuss controversial subjects.

5. Be a name-dropper.

6. Interrupt.

7. Make a decision to accept the job immediately upon getting an offer.

8. Accept an offer before you have completed all of your interviews.

9. Renege on a job offer.

10. Smoke unless the interviewer smokes.

11. Take other people with you to the interview.

12. Use profanity.

13. Be overbearing.

14. Condemn former employers, faculty or associates.

15. Place too much emphasis on salary and benefits at the beginning of an interview.

16. Express biases or prejudices.

17. Present a poor resume.

18. Be negative.

Additional Tips When Interviewing

During the course of the interview there are little responses that can sometimes make a difference and strike a positive chord with the interviewer.

When responding to a question, try to relate your course work or work experience to the question whenever appropriate. For example, if you have prepared a term paper related to a given question, work that into your response.

Leadership skills should be accented in your response, if appropriate. Relating some of your leadership responsibilities to a given job can have a very positive effect. If you have worked on team projects make sure that is known. If you have assumed special responsibilities, such as a Multiple Sclerosis Drive that you chaired, bring that into the conversation.

Anything that demonstrates sound work habits, dependability or perseverance add to the credentials that aren't on your resume and may be pursued by the interviewer.

Respond to questions positively. Beware of taking a negative approach in any response.

If you have attended seminars or conferences that have a particular relationship to the job you are seeking, bring those up. Faculty associations that were particularly valuable can be mentioned. If you had any mentors, you might want to mention them.

Give the impression that you want to continue learning by going to grad school while on the job, attending professional meetings or by subscribing to certain journals to indicate your professional approach to your career.

Don't be afraid to express your ideas as they pertain to the job. Stay away from religious, political and controversial subjects.

Convey the fact that you are realistic in your career aspirations and that you are looking for that employer who is fair and has opportunities for those willing to contribute.

Most recruiters subscribe to the theory that past behavior, performance, and achievement are the best indicators of future behavior, performance, and achievement. Once you recognize and accept this approach by the recruiter, you will respond to interview questions with this in mind.

Coupling this with any advance information you acquire on the job description, company, products, and recent media information (mergers, profit picture, etc.) can make a difference in your responses. The main idea, then, is to relate your background and education to those factors.

This does not mean you mislead or misstate your qualifications. It means you relate your background and experiences to what the recruiter is looking for.

Some Special Considerations

How Do Employers View the Grade Point Average?

How to handle questions regarding grade point average is a common problem for many students. Dr. Patrick Scheetz of the Collegiate Employment Research Institute at Michigan State University asked for comments on this subject from recruiters visiting campuses.

According to employers, grade point averages are merely one of many indicators of success on the job. Other important factors in their evaluations were how well-balanced the individual was and the total college experience.

Some organizations have a minimum of 3.0 (on 4.0 scale). Public accounting firms seem to put more emphasis on GPA than other areas of employment. Many organizations in the technical disciplines believe there is a high correlation between grade point average and intelligence according to the survey. In sales and personnel, high grade point averages have not been an accurate measure of success according to many employers.

My personal experience in seeing students with high and low GPA's is that there is little correlation between GPA and success in business. A GPA at one college or university may be an entirely different standard from that of another institution. Departments within colleges have different criteria for giving grades as do professors within a given department.

If you are going to pursue an advanced degree in medicine, law, higher education or high tech occupations, a high GPA is a decided advantage. For graduating seniors planning to enter the employment market there are many other factors that are important when employers make their hiring decision. For example, people skills are very important in almost any field you choose (most people who are terminated from a job are terminated for lack of people skills than for lack of technical skills). Common sense, appreciation of the work ethic, good written and spoken skills, motivation, integrity and problem solving skills all are very important.

There have been numerous surveys on GPA and future success on the job. Some employers have found that there is a correlation between success on the job and GPA but many others have found there to be no correlation between the two. The larger corporations, in my experience, put more emphasis on the importance of GPA than the smaller ones.

If you have a low GPA and find you are rejected by an employer because of that reason, don't worry. There are plenty of other employers who will be happy to consider you for the other skills.

What about Students Who Have Military Reserve Status?

Most organizations have policies with guaranteed employment for military reservists who are activated during a national emergency. Some employers are not aware of federal laws covering this situation. Should this become a subject of discussion in an interview, refer to Chapter 43 of the U.S. Code, Title 38, which states that reservists and national guard personnel who are called to active duty during a national emergency have "protected status." This law is also known as the Military Leave Act.

Should You Accept a Job for Which You Are Overqualified?

Some employers say this may be the only way into some organizations. This can be especially true in times of a recession or for students in low demand disciplines. The answer depends on your financial status, your interests, your potential and the potential of the job offer.

Employers say high performers will be recognized in the long run once they demonstrate their abilities and willingness to work. Many organizations have policies of promoting only from within. Since vacancies are not generally open to the public, this is the only way, sometimes, to join a company. Moving within a company is usually much easier than coming in from an outside organization.

Traditionally, some majors in communication arts, marketing, fisheries and wildlife, advertising, tourism, history, romance languages and other disciplines have found it advantageous to accept a job for which they are overqualified.

For many, it beats having no job at all!

What If You're Not a "Perfect" Candidate?

In this country, if you are willing to work and respect the work ethic you can succeed. You can be lacking in many skills and abilities, but if you can demonstrate that you want to work and will work hard, there are many employers who will hire you.

Many recruiters feel some college graduates are not willing to "pay the price" the employers are looking for. Employers say too many recent graduates want to start at the top without the requirements necessary to succeed. Some have said the education process has been too easy on them and they have been too protected from making it on their own. Old fashioned ideas? Maybe so, but more and more employers are putting emphasis on co-op programs, internships, summer employment, part time work (career related) and those factors that indicate discipline and self-reliance.

Another spin-off of these "old fashioned" ideas is that of commitment. Employers believe that commitment to an employer is fading fast. Seniors think in terms of one, two or maybe three years of working for an employer unless they see themselves on a fast track in the organization. This concept was partially brought about by the rapid growth of business, industry and government in the 70's and 80's, where people moved upward rapidly if they demonstrated potential. That growth has temporarily been slowed down, thus the vacancies up the ladder are much fewer.

So, when you have your interviews, be aware of these factors when talking with the person doing the hiring. He or she may be just "old fashioned" enough to see the importance of these factors and decide on whether to make an offer to you depending on how you look at these matters.

chapter three

The Campus Recruiting Process

The career planning and placement office is the bridge between the world of education and the world of work. The services offered by universities and colleges vary greatly, but most institutions have basic services such as career counseling, a career library, and the opportunity for on-campus interviewing between students and employers. In addition, many colleges and universities offer workshops, credential referral services, courses in career planning, resume design assistance, alumni contacts, supply and demand information, employer address lists, and starting salary data. Take advantage of these services because once you have graduated and leave the campus, these services are much more difficult to obtain. Personal interviews are particularly more difficult to obtain after you leave campus.

Learn About the Placement System Operations

Adequate preparation before the campus interview is extremely important. Talk to the placement director to become familiar with all the services available. Provide ample time in your senior year to schedule interviews. Faculty and placement personnel are excellent sources of information about employers and their needs.

Questions for recruiters should be prepared in advance of interviewing. Some interviewers will ask candidates if they have any questions. At that point, students should be prepared to take the offensive and ask specifics about the employer's job opportunities, organizational policies and living conditions. If you should be seeking a teaching position, inquire about support personnel, school policies, employment benefits, community support and living conditions in the surrounding geographical area.

Students majoring in technical subjects will usually find more employers visiting campuses than nontechnical graduates. Liberal arts graduates, for example, may not be able to get as many on-campus interviews as engineers, but liberal arts graduates can find many leads by networking and personal contacts. The career planning library usually has a wealth of information on job search strategies, including interviewing, so avail yourself of those opportunities.

Signing up for interviews can be very competitive. Knowing the rules and capabilities of the placement office operation can sometimes help you get on interviewing schedules that would otherwise not be available to you. Computerized interview sign-up systems can sometimes permit last-minute appointments for schedules that originally were filled. "No shows" happen, and if you know the system, you can sometimes substitute at the last minute.

Meet and Know the Placement Officer at Your School

Knowing the placement personnel at your college or university can be very valuable in your job search and when arranging campus interviews. Personnel in this office can help you handle interviews and answer questions asked by recruiters. They can provide starting salary information and give you an idea of your approximate market value. They can provide reference materials and steer you in the right direction during the on-campus and off-campus interviewing processes.

Sometimes when talking with employers, the placement officer is asked to recommend someone for a particular job. If the placement officer knows you, he or she might identify you as an excellent prospect. Support from friends and relatives can be very helpful when finding a job, but quite often, the key person in the recruitment process is the placement officer at your university.

This brings up another important point. Much of the success of an interview is dependent upon the work you accomplish with others *prior* to the interview. Keep key people apprised of your job status during the interviewing process. By doing this, these important people can frequently add suggestions that will help you.

Many students may be reluctant to contact their placement officers, friends or relatives when it comes to the job hunt. They believe they can get a job by themselves—until it is too late. Most people can be contacted and are willing to lend a helping hand to inexperienced job seekers with advice, suggestions, and leads for interviews. This is all part of the networking process that leads to success.

Be Familiar with the Career Planning Library

The career planning library can be a most important source of information. Take advantage of this resource: it is a major element when planning an effective interview. The resources are almost limitless.

Information on file in the career planning library includes a broad range of self-help and job search books in addition to considerable information on job interviewing. Here are but a few examples:

Pre-interviewing information on employers can be obtained from company brochures, professional directories, *Standard and Poor's* directories, *Moody's*, and *Dun and Bradstreet* publications. Nonprint media are also becoming a larger part of career information centers. These include video tapes or laser disc systems plus audio and video tapes on interviewing.

Individual descriptions of jobs, career fields, and industries including supply-demand and salary information (i.e., *Dictionary of Occupational Titles* and *Annual Salary Reports*) are often included.

Self-help materials especially designed for women, minorities, and the handicapped (*I Can Be Anything: A Career Book for Women*, *The Black Resources Guide*, and *Minority Student Opportunities in U.S. Medical Schools, 1990–91* can be helpful. Career planning aids (*College to Career: Finding Yourself in the Job Market*, and *What Color is Your Parachute? A Practical Guide for Job Hunters and Career Changers, 1991*) will get you started.

Salary information (*College Placement Council Salary Survey* and *Recruiting Trends*) are also available and can help you estimate your economic worth on the job market. It's important to have this information at your fingertips so you better understand your situation and can negotiate your salary needs.

The reference librarian at a public library can also be an excellent resource person for finding answers to specific questions to meet your special needs.

Take the time to conduct in-depth research on the organizations you intend to interview. Gather as much information as you can on the people, their products, the organization, and its financial health. This information will considerably enhance your employment potential.

Learn the Current Job Market for Graduates in Your Discipline

The job market for new college graduates changes from year to year. Witness the change in supply and demand for graduates during the 1982–83 and 1990–91 recessions. Even the supply of graduates changes from year to year. (See Chart A).

CHART A

Bachelor's Degrees Expected by Sex of Recipient			
Year	*Total*	*Men*	*Women*
1991–92	1,060,000	503,000	557,000
1992–93	1,063,000	506,000	557,000
1993–94	1,058,000	506,000	552,000
1994–95	1,047,000	502,000	545,000
1995–96	1,031,000	497,000	534,000
1996–97	1,015,000	493,000	522,000
1997–98	1,012,000	496,000	516,000
1998–99	1,010,000	499,000	511,000
1999–2000	1,019,000	508,000	511,000
2000–2001	1,037,000	522,000	515,000

National Center for Education Statistics. 1990. *Projections of Education Statistics to 2001*. Washington, D.C.: U.S. Department of Education, Office of Educational Research and Improvement. pp. 52.

There has been a prevailing view by some recent college graduates that once you receive a degree, the jobs are there for the taking. However, thousands of graduating students have found this to be a myth. Regardless of the year in which you graduate, there is substantial competition, especially in the lesser demand disciplines such as liberal arts, communications, social sciences, advertising, philosophy and religion.

The important point is this: you are *one* person who needs *one* job. Learn all you can about your competition and the job market, develop a positive attitude, be persistent, properly develop your job campaigning strategies—and you will find your way.

The pattern of academic majors in demand among college graduates seeking employment over the past decade has been relatively unchanged. For example, engineering, nursing, computer and information services, sales, and the physical sciences have had the most favorable supply/demand ratio (See Chart B). The future continues to bode well for these disciplines.

Health careers over the next decade will offer enormous opportunities due to an aging population requiring more hospital-

CHART B

Estimated Job Demand by Field of Study
1991–92
Bachelor's Degree Graduates

Academic Majors	Estimated Numbers	Percent of Total
FAVORABLE SUPPLY/DEMAND RATIO		
Business and Management	259,668	24.50%
Engineering	74,168	7.00%
Health Professions	64,126	6.05%
Computer and Information Sciences	36,866	3.48%
Engineering Technologies	20,580	1.94%
Physical Sciences	18,968	1.79%
Total Graduates—	474,376	44.75%
COMPETITIVE SUPPLY/DEMAND RATIO		
Education	97,118	9.16%
Mathematics	16,954	1.60%
Protective Services	14,266	1.35%
Architecture and Environmental Design	9,183	0.87%
Communications Technologies	1,412	0.13%
Other	3,816	0.36%
Total Graduates—	142,749	13.47%
VERY COMPETITIVE SUPPLY/DEMAND RATIO		
Social Sciences	106,996	10.09%
Communications	48,426	4.57%
Psychology	47,977	4.53%
Letters	42,153	3.98%
Life Sciences	39,227	3.70%
Visual and Performing Arts	39,055	3.68%
Liberal/General Studies	23,258	2.19%
Multi/Interdisciplinary Studies	18,531	1.75%
Home Economics	15,820	1.49%
Public Affairs	15,187	1.43%
Agriculture and Natural Resources	15,176	1.43%
Foreign Languages	10,701	1.01%
Philosophy and Religion	6,359	0.60%
Theology	5,959	0.56%
Parks and Recreation	4,355	0.41%
Area and Ethnic Studies	3,695	0.35%
Total Graduates—	442,875	41.78%
GRAND TOTAL—All Fields	1,060,000	

Sources: Supply/demand ratios and numbers of graduates estimated by John D. Shingleton, Director Emeritus of Placement Services, and L. Patrick Scheetz, Director of the Collegiate Employment Research Institute, Michigan State University. Grand total of bachelor's degree recipients from *Projections of Education Statistics to 2001*, published by the National Center for Education Statistics, U.S. Department of Education, Washington, D.C., 1990, p. 52.

ization and health care services. This occupational area has the potential for the fastest growth according to the U.S. Department of Labor statistics. The second fastest growing occupation requiring a skill is computer programming, which has spin-off applications in other areas of employment, such as accounting and engineering. Demand for engineers will not diminish greatly, in the long run, even though demand fluctuates from year to year.

Education, mathematics, protective services, architecture and communication technologies majors will usually have job opportunities, but graduates in these majors will have to work at their job hunting to be successful.

An important indicator of the supply/demand ratio for various disciplines is the diverse range of starting salary offers. Anticipated starting salary offers for different academic majors in the 1991–92 school year are provided in Chart C.

As would be expected, new graduates in health services, technical fields and science majors are expected to receive the highest starting salaries. Engineers, for example, will average about $34,000 a year to start in 1992. At the other end of the spectrum, advertising, retailing, telecommunications, human ecology, natural resources and journalism majors will find starting salaries, on average, in the $20,000 to $22,000 range.

When interviewing with prospective employers, there are many factors that go into a successful interview. A very important matter is understanding the economics of the job market, for this is the reality of the situation.

Hiring Expectations of Employers

In 1990–91, the Collegiate Employment Research Institute surveyed the expectations of employers hiring recent college graduates in the coming year. Practically all of these employers visited campuses to interview college graduates. Over five hundred employers from business, industry, governmental agencies and educational institutions responded to the survey.

CHART C

Estimated Starting Salaries
of 1991–92

New Bachelor's Degree Graduates

Academic Majors	*Estimated Average Starting Salary*
Chemical Engineering	$38,394
Mechanical Engineering	$35,555
Electrical Engineering	$34,917
Computer Science	$32,706
Industrial Engineering	$32,774
Physics	$29,724
Nursing	$29,159
Civil Engineering	$29,824
Chemistry	$28,105
Accounting	$27,195
Financial Administration	$25,382
Geology	$28,776
Mathematics	$27,835
General Business Admin.	$25,635
Marketing/Sales	$26,124
Personnel Administration	$22,953
Agriculture	$22,702
Social Science	$21,674
Communications	$22,107
Liberal Arts/Arts & Letters	$21,667
Education	$23,402
Hotel, Rest. Inst. Mgt.	$22,570
Advertising	$22,194
Retailing	$20,030
Telecommunications	$22,434
Human Ecology/Home Economics	$20,658
Natural Resources	$21,776
Journalism	$20,079

Source: Estimates by John D. Shingleton, Director Emeritus of Placement Services, and L. Patrick Scheetz, Director of the Collegiate Employment Research Institute, Michigan State University, using data from *Recruiting Trends 1990-91.*

When responding to the question, "In your organization (1990–91), what types of positions are likely to be available to new college graduates?" they responded:

Account executive
Account manager—
   assistant
Account management
   trainee
Accounts receivable clerk
Accountant—assistant,
   associate
Accounting assistant
Accounting trainee
Actuary
Administrative assistant
Administrative trainee
Advertising sales rep
   trainee
Aerospace engineer
Aerospace technologist
Agricultural engineer
Agronomy sales
   representative
Analyst—associate
Applications engineer—
   associate
Architect
Artist
Audit staff member
Audit and business advisor
Auditor—associate
Automotive engineer
Banker development
   management associate
Banking center manager
Benefits assistant
Biologist

Boutique manager
Branch clerk
Branch manager
Business advisor
Business administrator
Business systems analyst
Business systems
   consultant
Buyer—assistant,
   associate
CAD designer
CAD engineer
Cartographer
Case manager
Chemical engineer
Chemical process engineer
Chemist
Chief building inspector
Civil engineer
Claims adjuster
Claims representative
Collection specialist
Commercial banker
Commercial lending
   banker
Computer analyst
Computer engineer
Computer programmer
Computer scientist—
   associate
Computer technician
Configuration
   management analyst
Construction inspector

Construction manager

Construction
superintendent—
assistant

Consulting engineer

Consultant

Controls engineers

Controller trainee

Controlling assistant

Corporate financial
analyst

Corporate lending
specialist

Corporate specialty
service worker

Corrections counselor

Corrective therapist

Corrosion engineer

Corrosion technician

Cost analyst

Credit analyst

Credit representative

Criminal investigator

Crop production specialist

Curator

Customer relations rep

Customer service rep

Customer support
engineer

Deli assistant

Design engineer

Development engineer

Die engineer

Dietitian

Dining room supervisor

Director of nursing

Distribution specialist

District Attorney—
assistant

Division engineer

Draftsperson

Drilling engineer

Electrical design engineer

Electrical engineer—
associate

Employment/placement
coordinator

Employment supervisor

Engineer—assistant,
associate

Engineering assistant

Engineering trainee

Environmental engineer

Equipment engineer

Evaluation engineer

Facility engineer

Farm production manager

Feed sales representative

Field accountant

Field chemist

Field engineer

Field representative

Field service
representative

Field service engineer

Field technician

Finance director—
assistant

Financial analyst

Financial management
specialist

Food service management
trainee

Forensic chemist

Front desk manager
trainee
Front office shift leader
Front office manager
General management
trainee
General office assistant
Geographer
Geological engineer
Geologist
Graphics engineer
Grain merchandiser
Grocery store assistant
Hardware engineer
Health administrator
Health physicist
Highway designer
Horticulturist
Hospitality & restaurant
management trainee
Hotel management trainee
Housekeeping manager
trainee
Human resources trainee
Human service worker
Hydrogeologist
Industrial designer
Industrial engineer
Industrial sales trainee
Information center
consultant—associate
Information specialist
Information systems
specialist
Inside sales representative
Internal sales
representative
Internal auditor

Junior engineer
Junior industrial engineer
Junior logistic engineer
Laboratory
administrator—assistant
Laboratory technician
Landscape architect
Lawyer
Livestock production
specialist
Logistics management
specialist
Loss prevention associate
Loss prevention
representative
Machine design engineer
Manager trainee
Manager; assistant
manager
Management information
consultant
Management intern
Management trainee
Manufacturing interface
engineer
Manufacturing engineer—
associate
Marketing visual
merchandiser
Marketing analyst
Marketing associate
Marketing representative
Marketing support
representative
Materials engineer
Materials inspector
Materials management
Mathematician—associate

Measurement engineer
Mechanical designer
Mechanical engineer—
associate
Medical technologist
Medical researcher
Network systems engineer
New business clerk
New staff consultant
Newspaper reporter
Night manager
Nurse
Nursing home
administrator
Nutritionist
Occupational therapist
Office manager—assistant
Operational analysis
engineer
Operations supervisor
Outpatient therapist
Paralegal
Packaging engineer—
associate
Packing house manager
Personnel representative
Petroleum engineer
Pharmacist
Photographer
Photography trainee
Physical therapist
Physicist—associate
Planning engineer
Plant engineer
Plant project engineer
Plastics engineer
Police officer
Policy analyst

Power service engineer
Practical nurse
Private banking
representative
Process engineer
Product development
engineer
Production control analyst
Production engineer
Production planner
Production manager—
assistant
Programmer/analyst
Project accountant—
assistant
Project engineer
Project manager trainee
Proposal engineer
Psychologist
Purchasing agent
Purchasing assistant
Quality assurance analyst
Quality control trainee
Quality engineer
Radiology technician
Real estate banking
representative
Recreation administrator
Recreation therapist
Regulator specialist
Reliability engineer
Reporter
Reporter trainee
Researcher
Research analyst
Research & development
engineer—associate
Research assistant

Research chemist
Research engineer
Research technician
Reservoir engineer
Respiratory therapist
Restaurant manager
Restaurant manager
   trainee
Retail supervisor
Risk scientist
Robotics engineer
Scientist—associate

Staff member—associate
Transportation specialist
Trust manager
Trust & securities rep
Trust services rep
Ultrasound technologist
Underwriter
Unit manager—assistant
Video journalist
Water resource planner
Writer

Liberal Arts Degree Candidates and the Job Market

The survey mentioned in the preceding pages also asked the question "If your organization hires new college graduates with liberal arts degrees, to what positions are they usually assigned?"

Many liberal arts graduates are not aware of the many job opportunities that liberal arts graduates fill. Here is the list the employers provided in answering the question:

Accountant/cost
   accountant
Administrative assistant/
   trainee/specialist/
   coordinator/officer
Advertising account
   executive
Agricultural marketing
   specialist
Artist assistant
Assistant account manager
Auditor/auditing
   consultant

Bank branch manager
Bank development
   management associate
Benefits assistant
Branch clerk
Business system analyst
Cartographer
Child support enforcement
   officer
Claims examiner
Collections specialist
Communications
   assistant

Community banking
trainee
Computer specialist/
analyst trainee
Contract associate/
specialist
Corporate communications
officer
Counselor/corrections
counselor
Credit representative/
analyst
Customer services/
relations rep
Direct care worker
Economic development
officer
Employee development
specialist
Employee relations
specialist
Employee trainer
Energy management
specialist
Engineering planner/
trainee
Field representative
Financial planner/
consultant
Food and beverage
manager
Front office manager
Graphic designer
Historical property
curator
Industrial designer
Legal paraprofessional/
preprofessional

Management analyst/
trainee
Manager/management
trainee/associate
Marketing rep/associate/
assistant
Museum assistant
Museum education
coordinator
Museum exhibit technician
New business clerk
New staff consultant
Office administrator
Operations assistant
Outpatient therapist
Personnel trainee/rep
Photographer
Planning/scheduling
coordinator
Product administrator
Program supervisor
Programmer
Public relations rep
Purchasing/procurement
assistant
Research analyst/research
assistant
Residential unit manager/
assistant manager
Restaurant assistant
manager
Restaurant manager
Retail assistant manager
Retail manager trainee
Sales representative/
assistant
Sales territory manager
Secretary

Securities associate
Social work case manager
System analyst
Human resource officer/
  rep
Plant project engineer
Plastics engineer
Police officer
Policy analyst
Power service engineer
Private banking
  representative
Process engineer
Product development
  engineer
Production control analyst
Production engineer
Production planner
Production management
Programmer/analyst
Project engineer
Project manager trainee
Proposal engineer
Psychologist
Purchasing agent
Purchasing assistant
Quality assurance agent
Quality control trainee
Quality engineer
Radiology technician
Real estate banking
  representative
Recreation administrator
Recreation therapist
Regulator specialist
Reliability engineer
Reporter

Reporter trainee
Researcher
Research & development
  engineer
Research chemist
Research engineer
Research technician
Reservoir engineer
Respiratory therapist
Risk scientist
Robotics engineer
Rotational engineer
Sales counselor
Sales engineer
Sales manager/trainee
Sales promotion
  representative
Sales representative/
  trainee
Scientist
Scientist's assistant
Senior analyst
Service engineer
Shift supervisor
Showroom trainee
Social services worker
Social worker
Software analyst
Software developer
Software engineer
Speech pathologist
Special events assistant
Statistician
Staff accountant
Store manager
Stress engineer
Structural designer

Structural engineer
Substance abuse
  counselor
Supervisor
Supervisor trainee
Systems analyst
Systems engineer
Tax consultant
Tax professional
Tax services specialist
Technical aid
Technical training
  instructor
Technical sales rep
Technical specialist
Technical staff assistant
Technical staff engineer

Technician
Technical writer
Territory manager
Test engineer
Tool engineer
Tool/machine designer
Traffic coordinator
Transportation specialist
Trust manager
Trust & securities rep
Trust services rep
Ultrasound technologist
Underwriter
Unit manager
Video journalist
Water resource planner
Writer

Employment Growth Categories

When employers in the survey were asked "What job categories in your organization are experiencing the most growth in employment?" there was particular emphasis on technical sciences, computer related fields and customer service jobs.

Here are their responses by job title:

Accelerator engineer
Accountant/auditor/tax
  analyst
Attorney/hearing officer
Bank branch manager/
  trainee
Bridge engineer
CAD/CAM drafting
  technicians
Chemical engineer

Chemist
Civil engineer
Commercial lending
  officer
Communications
  technician
Computer process control
  engineer
Computer programmer
Computer scientist

Construction engineer
Consulting engineer
Corrections security
  officer
Corrections counselor
Customer services
  representative
Data communications
  specialist
Data processing tech/
  operator
Design engineer
Electrical engineer
Engineering technician
Environmental engineer
Feed sales representative
Financial analyst
Food and beverage worker
Grain merchandiser
Graphic designer
Hotel manager/trainee
Human resources manager
Import/export specialist
Landscape architect
Management trainee
Manufacturing engineer
Marketing/sales
  representative
Mathematician
Mechanical engineer
Medical technologist
Metallurgical engineer
Mining engineer
Newspaper designer
Nuclear engineer
Nuclear technician

Nurse
Occupational therapist
Pharmacist
Physical therapist
Physicist
Production supervisor
Production worker
Project manager/
  superintendent
Radiation therapy
  technician
Radiology technician
Research and development
  engineer
Restaurant manager/
  trainee
Retail store manager/
  trainee
Robotics engineer
Sales engineer
Software/applications
  engineer
Special events manager
Systems development
  engineer
Systems analyst
Store operations manager/
  trainee
Technical agribusiness
  manager
Technical sales rep
Telecommunications
  specialist
Telemarketing
  representative
Thermal engineer

Qualities Sought in Candidates by Employers

It is important to recognize and understand those special qualities sought by employers in order to avoid being turned down for the wrong reasons. Many recruiters, sorry to say, spend a large share of the interview time looking for reasons to turn you down—not a very positive approach to selection of personnel, but a hard, cold fact of the employment process. You may have many glowing characteristics but if there is a flaw to be found that the interviewer finds negative, look out!

Given that as a possibility, a survey of employers was made by the Collegiate Employment Research Institute to find the qualities most sought after by employers in business, industry and government. The importance of these qualities varied with the employer and, of course, some were more important than others. Chart D is a sampling of those qualities ranked by importance according to the employers reporting.

Final Tips

It is very easy to adopt a cavalier attitude to arranging interviews and finding a job while attending college. There are so many other things to occupy your time during you senior year that procrastination can easily occur.

This has proven to be a big mistake for many college students. Missed opportunities occurred by not signing up for interviews at the placement office or failing to attend career planning events meant employment contacts never arranged.

Admittedly, such efforts require entering an unknown territory, so other activities are given a higher priority. To avoid this pitfall, begin by recognizing that you, and you alone, are responsible for arranging interviews and planning your career. Don't expect others (placement office staff, faculty, relatives, family) to perform the necessary tasks for you. And, above all, don't expect the job to come to you.

CHART D

Qualities Desired in New College Graduates
By Businesses, Industries, and Governmental Agencies

Always Important:

Dependability
Honesty and integrity
Ability to get things done
Desire to accept responsibility
Intelligence
Common sense
Problem-solving skills
Interpersonal skills
Mental stability
Maturity

Usually Important:

Self-confidence/poise
Decision-making abilities
Ambition
Flexibility/adaptability to change
Creative thinking skills
Motivational abilities
Leadership skills
Neatness of appearance
Diplomacy/tactfulness
Speaking abilities
Perseverance
Staying power and stability with
    an organization
Possession of self-pride
An excellent example for others
Writing skills
Innovative ideas
Time management skills

Competitive abilities
Mathematical skills
Team management skills
Ability to "go along" with an
    organization's way of doing
    things
Computer literacy

*Important, Depending Upon
Job:*

Tactical and strategic planning
    skills
Willingness to relocate
Entrepreneurial spirit
Physical fitness
Ability to delegate to others
Willingness to continue their
    education
Interest in current events
Candidate's prior knowledge of
    an organization
Budgeting abilities
Financial planning skills
Ability to work in close quarters
Attitudes toward their own
    family

Selectively Important:

Foreign language competencies
Overseas travel interests

Sheetz, L. Patrick. 1990. *Recruiting Trends 1990–91.* East Lansing, MI.: Collegiate
Employment Research Institute, Michigan State University.

Workshops, Career Fairs and Employment Seminars

You can learn much about your competition, employers, interviewing techniques, and making contacts by attending workshops, career fairs and seminars. Talk to employer participants in these events, because doors will be opened beyond your wildest dreams. Be prepared for a quick interview, with a possible in-depth interview later. Through these programs, many placement counselors are assisting in the placement of hundreds of graduates into jobs.

Your Credentials File

Strange as it may seem, many college students do not complete their credentials for a file in the placement office. Sometimes, those who complete the forms are apt to prepare them in a shoddy manner or some forms are not completed to the student's best advantage. Hard to believe? Not really! It happens all the time.

The items in a credentials file will vary from school to school, but all generally contain an official copy of your transcript(s), an information form, and several letters of recommendation. Your career planning office will assist you in setting up your credentials file.

Let Faculty Know of Your Availability

Faculty frequently meet and talk to employers. These employers often seek recommendations from faculty for jobs that are available. Get to know your professors and make them aware of your availability. You might even talk to them about employment, seek their advice, and leave a resume with them should an employer contact them for candidates to recommend.

Many employers rely heavily on faculty recommendations, and you should, during an employment interview, refer to faculty who would be willing to provide additional information on your college experiences.

The best way to cultivate faculty is to think of them as friends or mentors who are willing to help you. These faculty can be immensely helpful at graduation time with decision-making advice, recommendations, employer contacts, etc. Do not wait until a crisis occurs, however, to seek their help. Cultivate their relationship through course work, seminars and other meetings of mutual interest as you pursue your education.

chapter four

The On-Site Interview with Prospective Employers

You have been screened during the campus interview and found to be a possible candidate for employment, so you are invited to the job site for further interviewing. Prepare carefully for these interviews because you will now be evaluated by your prospective boss and co-workers. Do not assume the job is yours just because you have been invited to visit. Most employers invite more candidates for these interviews than they have jobs available, so they can select from the best candidates.

What to Expect

The on-site interview provides you with an opportunity to evaluate your potential employer, co-workers, job environment, and living conditions. Be sure you prepare a list of questions in advance regarding the whole employment scenario, since it is these interviews that will most likely help you make your decision to accept or reject the job—if it is offered. These interviews may be individual sessions or group interviews, or both. Be prepared for almost anything in these sessions.

Before accepting an invitation to a site visit, be sure all details regarding your expenses and reimbursement are understood. If you are visiting several organizations on one trip, advise them of your plans and suggest that expenses be split among the various employers.

Usually the interviewing schedule is very arduous and quite demanding for most new college graduates. Get a good night's rest the evening before the interviewing session. As you proceed with these interviews, think: Would I enjoy working here? Does this organization seem well organized and prosperous? How do the employees and the boss strike me? Try to get into the "culture" of the organization. Attempt to view yourself in this organization with your values, interests, and aptitudes.

The interviewers will vary greatly. Some are trained; some are not. Some seem friendly; some seem officious. Chances are, most of the on-site interviewers will have the campus recruiter's evaluation of you in hand. These interviewers will be more knowledgeable about the organization and the particular job you are seeking, generally, than the campus recruiter; their questions will be more specific and more pragmatic. This is the best time to get solid information on all details of the job, the bosses' expectations, your future potential, your competition, your benefits, and the quality of life you can expect in this organization.

Your schedule during this visit might be something like the one shown in Chart A.

Kinds of Interviews

After the initial screening interview which is usually of short duration, you may encounter any one of several interviewing methods during the on-site visit.

One-on-one interview.   The one-on-one personal interview by an employment staff member or line person usually begins the on-site interviewing process. The contents of this interview will usu-

CHART A

ABC Corporation Interview Schedule for
John James

TIME	PERSON	TITLE	AREAS TO BE COVERED
8:00 a.m.	Bill Robertson	Employment Manager	Plans for the day. Provide general company information. Explain expense account procedures.
9:00 a.m.	Stan Smith	Supervisor, Production	Explain the job, location, discuss candidate's background as it relates to job.
10:00 a.m.	Frank Beeman	Group Leader	Review credentials and academic work at university. Discuss interests of candidate. Provide information of technical nature regarding job. Review organizational chart especially as it relates to that unit.
11:00 a.m.	Fred Stafford Gordon Osborn Ed Fritz	Senior Engineers	Group interview—Questions coming from any of the interviewers covering any subject. Object is to get consensus opinion of candidate from that group.
12:00 p.m.	Lunch-Robertson, Smith, Beeman		To discuss interview to date. Determine how you handle yourself in social atmosphere.
1:30 p.m.	Art Mooney	Asst. Employment Mgr.	Tour facilities. Sometimes living areas included in this tour and discussion of schools, housing, etc.
2:30 p.m.	Casius Street	Plant Manager	Opportunity for plant manager to look you over, ask a few questions and make known any reservations he may have.
3:00 p.m.	Bill Robertson	Employment Manager	Make final wrap-up, answer questions, explain follow-up procedure. Discuss general salary expectations, your preliminary interest and available starting date.
4:00 p.m.	Return home.		

*Sometimes tests are scheduled by some employers and are included during the on-site interview.

ally include your qualifications, the job requirements, and a review of the itinerary for the day. This should be a 50-50 exchange of information and should include both you and the interviewer asking and answering questions.

Group interview.   In the group interview situation, there will be two, three, or more company representatives asking questions and arriving at a consensus of your potential. It is easy for a recent college graduate to be intimidated in this situation, but relax and be yourself. This format is often used by search committees when seeking candidates for a job.

Structured interview.   The structured interview is usually handled by one interviewer, following a prescribed set of questions. This format is used when many interviewers are screening several candidates. This process supposedly provides a uniform set of responses for the decision-makers to consider. Again, be yourself and be honest.

Unstructured interview.   The unstructured interview includes open-ended questions regarding your education and experiences; it is usually free-flowing. During this type of interview, be sure all of your best points are made known before the interview is finished. Not all employer representatives are skilled at interviewing, so a lot of important information can be accidently omitted. In such cases, make sure you cover all the bases. Get your message across.

Situation interview.   During the situation interview, after a few preliminaries, the employer describes a situation or problem and asks how you would handle it. Take your time, make sure you understand the question, and respond. If you do not know the answer, simply state that fact or ask for further clarification of the problem.

Stress interview.   The stress interview is precisely what the name implies: a stress/response opportunity. During the stress interview the interviewer(s) asks questions and places you in certain circumstances to test your response to stressful conditions. Once you realize this is the situation, take your time, keep your cool and play the game.

Visit Your Work Area and Immediate Supervisor

It is not always possible, but whenever the opportunity presents itself be sure to get an interview with your immediate supervisor. The first boss you have is very important to your future success, since this person can place an indelible stamp on you.

Beware of going to work for a person when the "chemistry" is wrong. You can have good rapport with the personnel manager and the campus recruiter, but the key person is your immediate supervisor. A good boss can become your mentor and help you move within an organization and establish yourself.

It is also important to see your work area. Many students have accepted jobs only to find the work environment intolerable, and they have resigned because of this singular reason. The physical surroundings of your work area are important for your enjoyment on the job. Look around the work area before finalizing your plans.

Negotiations and Closure

This can be the most important phase of the interview and requires considerable skill in many cases.

Negotiations

First of all, hear the employer's position thoroughly before you begin to state your side. You may find the employer will offer more than you anticipated.

Next, be sure you understand your bargaining position. If you are the only candidate available for the available assignment, your position is much better than a situation with four or five others possessing comparable qualifications.

Next, come prepared—especially if you expect to negotiate a starting salary. Try to learn the starting salary others have been offered and be sure you know the minimum you will accept. In short, you must negotiate from a sound economic point of view. Just because you feel you are worth more is not an acceptable ne-

gotiating position. On the other hand, if you have strong support-
ing reasons for a higher starting salary, present them.

Understand the total economic package including benefits, bonuses, profit sharing, incentives, travel allowances and expenses
before closing a deal.

Finally, you are in a much better position to negotiate *before*
agreeing to employment than you are afterwards. Your bargaining position erodes once you have agreed to be hired.

Closure

Regardless of the interview you have—pre-screening by phone,
on-campus, or on-site—always conclude with a course of action
that you and/or the interviewer will take following the interview.
Too often the candidate leaves the interview not knowing his/her
status nor when to expect to hear from the interviewer.

So, at the conclusion of the interview, ask the interviewer
about the next step in the recruitment process. The decision may
be that "there is no interest on our part at this time but we will
keep your resume on file." This is a negative response but at least
you know where you stand with this employer.

The interviewer may want to refer your resume to various departments in the organization, and then if there is further interest, you will be contacted. You should ask approximately how
long will it be before a decision is reached.

If an on-site interview is expected next, request specifics (in
writing) so you can plan accordingly.

In short, there are many options that can occur after an interview and you should know the exact actions, and the probable
time frame that will be needed. This will relieve you of much
anxiety and help you in your planning.

Sometimes employers can lead you into a sense of anticipa-
tion, so you relax on your job search only to find that they don't
make an offer and you have passed up interviewing opportunities with other employers in the meanwhile. Do not fall into this
trap. Keep interviewing until you have an offer in hand and or in
writing—and have accepted it.

Once you receive and accept an offer you should notify other
employers who have made you offers and you should take no fur-

ther interviews. Your job campaign has come to a successful conclusion. At this time, inform your college placement office personnel of your acceptance of an employer's offer, so they can cease placement efforts on your behalf.

After the Interview

Reimbursement for Expenses

Always have an understanding (how much, which expenses) of reimbursement for expenses involving on-site interviews *before making the trip*. Most employers reimburse candidates for travel expenses if the employer invites them for an interview away from the campus.

If interviews are arranged off campus at your request and involve expenses, these expenses are usually borne by you. If you are from the midwest and call an employer in New York to arrange an interview, you will generally be expected to bear these expenses unless agreement has been reached on other arrangements in advance.

Some employers reimburse candidates at the end of the day upon completion of an on-site visit. Other organizations reimburse candidates shortly after the visit. Most provide airline tickets in advance, when appropriate. Many employers provide you with a detailed expense sheet to complete and return. In any case, keep close track of your expenses and receipts, and do not pad the expenses.

The Thank You Letter After an Interview

The importance of a genuine thank you letter cannot be overestimated. The letter should express a sincere, well-phrased appreciation for the opportunity to be considered for a given position.

First, it tells the interviewer of your interest in the job. It also reminds that person that you want to be remembered when making future decisions on candidates. It reaffirms your interest in the opportunity if the interviewer had any doubts of your inter-

CHART B

Employer Contact Log

DATE	CONTACT PHONE	COMPANY	ACTION TAKEN	FOLLOW UP DATE BY ME	COMMENTS
1/14	Scott Schultz 371/555-1234	Ford	Campus Interview Phone He will contact me in 10 days	1/25	Good possibilities.
1/18	Mary Smythe 313/555-3210	Exxon	Campus Interview Phone She will contact me if interested further	1/28	Iffy.
1/25	Scott Schultz	Ford	He wants plant visit—will set up for 3/16		
1/26	Jim Andrews 517/555-0642	XYZ Steel	Campus Interview		Not Interested.
3/5	Lori Jones 313/555-0610	ABC Advertising	Walk-in visit	None	No jobs!
3/6	Helen Snow 313/555-1212	Growers, Inc.	Walk-in visit. Left Application.		Left application.
3/16	Scott Schultz	Ford	Plant visit 3/23	They will call me in 10 days. Call 3/26.	Looks good.

est. It also expresses courtesy—too often lacking in day-to-day employment practices.

Thank you letters can be handwritten or typed and should be mailed two or three days after your interview. Mail letters to all who interviewed you.

Keep a Log of Your Interviews

For those having campus interviews resulting in several on-site visits, be sure to keep a log of each interview and maintain a schedule of on-site visits (See Chart B). This will help you keep track of your interviews and action taken at each.

Do not accept "expense paid" visits if you are not interested in employment with an organization. Nor should you accept expenses from two employers if you visited more than one employer on one trip. There have been instances of these events happening, and the student later regretted it, since the employers will contact faculty and/or the placement office staff and complain when this breach of ethics occurs.

chapter five

The Offer

No matter how thrilled you may be, do not immediately accept a position at the conclusion of an interview. Take at least 24 hours to think over all the terms of the offer. Accepting a job is a tremendous commitment; it plays a major role in the quality of your life and your future. Think of all the ramifications of this acceptance before making the decision. It is one of the most important of your life for it establishes a path that can have lifelong implications.

Also, you should discuss the offer with your spouse, family, or friends to make sure it fits before rendering the final answer.

It is wise to complete all interviews before accepting an offer. However, do not make an employer wait too long for your answer or the offer might be withdrawn. Complete your interviewing schedule. Make sure you have considered all the options before accepting an offer. Do not interview other employers after accepting an offer because reneging on a job acceptance can have serious ramifications, not to mention the embarrassment and stigma attached to such this unethical practice.

Evaluating and Accepting an Offer

On some great day, you may receive a letter something like the one following. Now comes the hard part: do you accept?

Evaluating Your Offer

Some find it expedient to prepare a written index for use when comparing an offer with other job options or with the ideal job they are seeking. A general form can be used for this purpose, to help you give thoughtful consideration to all the key factors in the job selection. A sample evaluation form follows.

Acceptance Procedure

Once you have made the decision to accept a position, there are several things you should ensure before this job offer is finalized:

1. Be sure the conditions of the offer and acceptance are in order and in writing. Oral agreements through interviews and phone conversations are part of the preliminary process, but before you complete the deal, it is important that the agreement is in writing.

2. Notify by letter or personally contact all those who have been involved in your job search. Inform them of your job acceptance. This notice should include faculty, friends, placement personnel, references and appropriate employer representatives who have made job offers so they will know your plans. This is not only common courtesy but a good business practice.

A sample job acceptance letter follows. Your letter should note that you are happy to accept the offer as stated in the notification letter. If you want to counter the employer's offer on some point, handle this request by telephone, if possible, so that you sense the response and can negotiate accordingly.

If an employer's offer is made by telephone, repeat the terms of the offer in your letter of acceptance.

Typical Job Offer Letter

ABC Corporation
Box 362
Ivanhoe, Kansas 34620

March 12, 1991

Ms. Jan Schultz
Random Hall
Western State University
Kansas City, Kansas 48814

Dear Ms. Schultz:

Thank you for visiting with us last week and discussing employment opportunities. All of us were impressed with your qualifications and would like to extend an offer to you for the position of Marketing Specialist in our Marketing Department in Los Angeles.

The salary would be $_____ per month and a starting date of August 1, 19__ would be acceptable to us as I understand that is your preferred starting date.

Enclosed is a physical examination form that should be completed by your physician and returned to us as soon as possible. Employment is contingent upon passing the physical examination. You will be reimbursed for this expense.

We will also reimburse you for your moving expenses from Kansas City to Los Angeles, California. A relocation expense sheet for that purpose is enclosed which also includes our policy on payment of these expenses.

It will be necessary for you to let us know your answer to this offer by May 15, 19__, or an earlier date, if possible.

We look forward to having you join us. If you have any questions, please call me at (563) 555-4569.

Sincerely,

John Hopkins
Salaried Personnel Manager
ABC Corporation

encl.

Evaluating Your Offer(s)

Job Evaluation Form

Job Characteristics	*Company Name*	*Rating*
1. Do I really want to perform this work?		1 2 3 4 5
2. What is my long-range potential with this company?		1 2 3 4 5
3. Do I like my immediate supervisor?		1 2 3 4 5
4. Is the location right for me?		1 2 3 4 5
5. Is this the best possible job for me at this time?		1 2 3 4 5
6. Does the "culture" of the company suit my personality?		1 2 3 4 5
7. Are there additional educational opportunities available with this organization?		1 2 3 4 5
8. Is my family happy with this choice?		1 2 3 4 5
9. What are the opportunities for advancement (short vs. long run)?		1 2 3 4 5
10. Is the benefit program of this organization adequate?		1 2 3 4 5
11. What is the fit of this working environment with my preferences?		1 2 3 4 5
12. Is the compensation package adequate for my lifestyle?		1 2 3 4 5
13. Other desires or preferences:		
List: _____		1 2 3 4 5
_____		1 2 3 4 5

*1 is top rating, 5 is worst

Sample Acceptance Letter

798 Chesterfield Drive
Rochester, Ohio 48612

Mr. Emanual Garcia
XYZ Corporation
Atlanta, GA 26412

Dear Mr. Garcia:

This will confirm my acceptance of the position of marketing analyst in the BOC Division of your company. I am delighted with the opportunity to join your organization and feel this matches my objectives precisely. I also feel certain I can make a significant contribution to the XYZ Corporation.

The arrangements for starting work as outlined in your letter of March 6, 19__ are entirely satisfactory. I will arrange for the medical examination and drug test and report to work at 8:00 a.m. on July 3, 19__ as stated. Enclosed are the forms you requested I fill out and return to you.

This promises to be a fine opportunity and I look forward to joining your company.

Sincerely,

Debra Benson

encl.

Thank the employer for the job offer and express your interest in reporting to work at the specified time and place. Include a paragraph on those aspects of the position that did, indeed, impress you.

Special Circumstances

Requesting delay in a job offer

When an offer is extended and you have other possibilities or interviews scheduled, you may want to explore those opportunities. In this situation, you should respond to the offer by explaining your reasons for requesting a delay in responding to the offer. By doing this, recognize that you may jeopardize your chances for employment, although most employers will usually give you a reasonable amount of time to make your decision.

In your response, refer to the employer's communication and the date. State that you are interested in their offer but you:

1. Would like to complete your schedule of interviews.

2. Request that more information is needed to make your decision.

3. Have personal reasons for the request. State the reasons you cannot make a decision at this time.

4. Propose a date for giving them an answer.

5. Request confirmation of this request.

If you discuss this matter by phone with the prospective employer, be sure to immediately confirm any verbal agreements by letter.

Declining an Offer

Being in the position of rejecting an offer requires tact. The matter should be handled courteously and promptly once the decision is made.

Of course, you will want to thank the employer for consideration, time, and effort. Use your own discretion if you want to inform the employer of the reason for declining. Some candidates mention the company they plan to join, but generally, this is not included.

In respectfully declining the offer, you may or may not give the reason(s). Avoid critical comments. Close this letter with an appreciative note and good wishes.

Finally, keep copies of all your correspondence with employers. Retain them for at least a year in case events turn out unexpectedly with the employer hiring you. If that should happen you might like to be considered at a later date by the rejected employer. This is a long shot, but has happened successfully a number of times in the past.

Thank You Letters

Even though you have accepted a job offer, it is simply good business practice and goodwill to write thank you letters to all the people who have been involved with your job finding efforts.

Be sure to write those employers whom you interviewed with and those who gave you advice during your job search. A note to those you listed as references would be wise also. This thoughtfulness is often neglected but will be appreciated and will distinguish you from other candidates. You may want to use these references or contacts at some time in the future.

When the Employer Doesn't Call

If you do not have a bona fide job offer *in hand*, do not immediately reject any offers. You may find that other offers are not

Sample Rejection Letter

Ms. Shirley Maott:
Research and Development Division
ABC Corporation
Boca Raton, FL 34617

Dear Ms. Maott:

Thank you for your consideration of my employment as an associate research engineer in your company. I have given a great deal of thought to the offer and have decided to decline the offer.

You have a fine organization and there are many aspects of the position that are appealing to me. At this time, however, I have decided on this course of action.

Once again, thanks for considering me and the many courtesies extended.

Very truly yours,

Kristin Mahoney

forthcoming and you will not want to burn any bridges until you have accepted a position. If you do, you may be sorry later.

During the interviewing process the interviewer will normally stipulate when he or she will contact you regarding the outcome of an interview. If the interviewer does not contact you by the date agreed, feel free to phone or personally contact that person. Wait two or three days past the stipulated date and then make the contact.

Continue to search for opportunities. Never cease your job search until you have an absolute offer and acceptance in hand. Don't assume goodwill equals an offer. The employment situation can change rapidly in any organization and, until you complete the whole deal, do not discontinue interviewing with other employers.

Closure on the Job Hunt

After the interviews, correspondence and negotiations, it is a good business practice to have a complete understanding of the offer and acceptance agreement. Such items as job title, job location, compensation, benefits, physical examination conditions (including drug testing), temporary housing allowances (if applicable), expenses (including travel and relocation), potential for graduate school financial support, starting date and time, and a multitude of other details should be received in writing and agreement should be reached by both parties. Many slip-ups occur because of misunderstandings during the interview that can be costly or embarrassing once you start on the job. Having the summary of your negotiations and interviews in written form can prevent these possibilities.

appendix a

Bibliography

Allen, Jeffrey G. *How to Turn an Interview into a Job*. New York: Simon & Schuster, Inc., 1983.

Billy, Christopher. *Peterson's Business and Management Jobs*. Princeton, N.J.: Peterson's Guides Inc., annual.

Billy, Christopher. *Peterson's Engineering, Science and Computer Jobs*. Princeton, N.J.: Peterson's Guides Inc., annual.

Bolles, Richard. *What Color is Your Parachute? A Practical Manual for Job Changers*. Berkeley, Calif.: Ten Speed Press, 1991.

Calhoun, Mary E. *How to Get Hot Jobs in Business and Finance*. New York: Harper and Row, Publishers Inc., 1988.

Conn, Steve and Paulo de Oliveira. *Getting to the Right Job*. New York: Workman Publishing Inc., 1987.

Consoli, Vivian. *Working Smart: A Woman's Guide to Starting a Career*. Glenview, Ill.: Scott, Foresman and Co., 1987.

Davison, Roger. *You Can Get Anything You Want*. New York: Simon and Schuster, 1987.

Erdlen, John D. and Donald H. Sweet. *Job Hunting for the College Graduate.* Lerington, Ma.: D.C. Heath and Co., 1979.

Figler, Howard. *The Complete Job-Search Handbook: All the Skills You Need to Get Any Job and Have a Good Time Doing It.* New York: Henry Holt and Co. Inc., 1988.

Figler, Howard. *Liberal Education and Careers Today.* Garret Park, Md.: Garret Park Press, 1989.

Fisher, Roger and William Ury. *Getting to Yes: Negotiating Agreement Without Giving in.* New York: Penguin Books, 1981.

Gerberg, Robert Jameson. *The Professional Job Changing System.* Performance Dynamics Inc., 1981.

Knight, Carol Rae. *Interview for Success: A Practical Guide to Increasing Job Interviews, Offers, and Salaries.* Virginia Beach, Va.: Impact Publications, 1990.

Knight, David M. *How to Interview for that Job—and Get It.* Connersville, Ind.: Knight Enterprises, 1976.

Lammon, Katherine R. *Job Search Techniques for Fine Artists: An Advisors Handbook.* California Institute of Fine Arts, 1985.

Lathrop, Richard. *Who's Hiring Who.* Berkeley, Calif.: Ten Speed Press, 1980.

Levin, Joel. *How to Get a Job in Education.* Holbrook, Mass.: Bob Adams, Inc., 1987.

Linquist, Carolyn Lloyd and Pamela F. Feodroff. *Where to Start Career Planning*, 7th ed. Princeton, N.J.: Peterson's Guides Inc., 1990–91.

Lobodinski, Jeanine, Deborah McFaddin, and Arlene Markowicz. *Marketing Your Abilities: A Guide for the Disabled Job-Seeker.*

Medley, H. Anthony. *Sweaty Palms Revised: The Neglected Art of Being Interviewed.* Belmont, Ca.: Lifetime Learning Publications, a division of Wadsworth Publishing Co., Inc., 1978.

Molloy, John T. *Dress for Success.* New York: Warner Books, Inc., 1975.

Molloy, John T. *The Women's Dress for Success Book*. New York: Warner Books, Inc., 1977.

Munschauer, John L. *Jobs for English Majors and Other Smart People*. Princeton, N.J.: Peterson's Guides Inc., 1986.

Nivens, Beatryce. *The Black Woman's Career Guide*. New York: Doubleday, 1987.

Petras, Rose and Kathryn. *The Only Job Hunting Guide You'll Ever Need*. New York: Simon & Schuster, 1989.

Scheetz, Patrick. *Recruiting Trends 1989-90. A Study of Businesses, Industries, Governmental Agencies, and Educational Institutions Employing New College Graduates*. East Lansing, MI: Michigan State University, annual.

Shingleton, John D. *Career Planning in the 1990's: A Guide for Today's Graduates*. Garrett Park, Md.: Garrett Park Press, 1991.

Shingleton, John D. and Robert Bao. *College to Career*. New York: McGraw-Hill Inc., 1977.

Snelling, Robert O. and Ann M. Snelling. *Jobs! What They Are... Where They Are... What They Pay*. New York: Simon & Schuster, 1989.

Steele, John E. and Marilyn S. Morgan. *Career Planning and Development for College Students and Recent Graduates*. Lincolnwood, Ill.: VGM Career Horizons, a division of NTC Publishing Group, 1991.

Thompson, Melvin R. *Why Should I Hire You?: Get the Job You Really Want*. Jove Publications, Inc., 1977.

appendix b

BUSINESS AND FINANCIAL DIRECTORIES

Career and corporate directories can help the job seeker identify possible employers. A list of some of the directories follows. Consult your local library for additional sources.

Career Employment Opportunity Directory
Ready Reference Press
Box 5169
Santa Monica, CA 90405
Published in four volumes: (1) Liberal Arts and Social Sciences, (2) Business Administration, (3) Engineering, (4) Sciences. Contains listing of companies currently hiring. Listings include employment opportunities, locations, and special programs.

Directory of Career Training & Development Programs
Ready Reference Press
Box 5169
Santa Monica, CA 90405
Lists management and executive training programs. List includes name, program title and purpose, number of people selected, type of training, qualifications, selection process, name and address of person to contact.

The Directory of Corporate Affiliations
National Register Publishing Co.
3004 Glenview Road
Wilmette, IL 60091
Includes profiles of over 4,000 U.S. companies, including subsidiaries, divisions, and affiliates.

Dun's Million Dollar Directory
Dun and Bradstreet
1 Pennsylvania Plaza
New York, NY 10013
The top 50,000 companies of the 160,000 listed in the *Million Dollar Directory*.
Listings include address, phone number, executive names, titles, and statistics.

Dun & Bradstreet's Reference Book of Corporate Management
99 Church Street
New York, NY 10013
Includes biographies of executives of top U.S. companies.

Moody's Industrial Manual
Moody's Investor Service, Inc.
99 Church Street
New York, NY 10013
Lists 3,000 companies on New York or American Stock Exchanges plus some international companies. Includes address, phone number, and statistics. Moody's also publishes directories on bank & finance, public utilities, transportation, and municipals.

Encyclopedia of Associations
Gale Research Co.
Book Tower
Detroit, MI 48226
Published in several volumes. Lists over 20,000 associations alphabetically by industry. An excellent kick-off point for networking. Available on line in DIALOG.

Standard and Poor's Register of Corporations, Directors and Executives
Standard and Poor's Corporation
345 Hudson Street
New York, NY 10014
Includes a massive list of corporations (45,000) and over 400,000 corporate officials. Volume 2 contains biographies of 75,000 executives and directors.

Career Placement Registry
302 Swan Avenue
Alexandria, VA 22301
Resume listing service. Cost is $12 for students, $45 for people in $40,000-and-up range.

VGM CAREER BOOKS

OPPORTUNITIES IN
*Available in both paperback and
  hardbound editions*
Accounting
Acting
Advertising
Aerospace
Agriculture
Airline
Animal and Pet Care
Architecture
Automotive Service
Banking
Beauty Culture
Biological Sciences
Biotechnology
Book Publishing
Broadcasting
Building Construction Trades
Business Communication
Business Management
Cable Television
Carpentry
Chemical Engineering
Chemistry
Child Care
Chiropractic Health Care
Civil Engineering
Cleaning Service
Commercial Art and Graphic Design
Computer Aided Design and
  Computer Aided Mfg.
Computer Maintenance
Computer Science
Counseling & Development
Crafts
Culinary
Customer Service
Dance
Data Processing
Dental Care
Direct Marketing
Drafting
Electrical Trades
Electronic and Electrical Engineering
Electronics
Energy
Engineering
Engineering Technology
Environmental
Eye Care
Fashion
Fast Food
Federal Government
Film
Financial
Fire Protection Services
Fitness
Food Services
Foreign Language
Forestry
Gerontology
Government Service
Graphic Communications
Health and Medical
High Tech
Home Economics
Hospital Administration
Hotel & Motel Management
Human Resources Management
  Careers
Information Systems
Insurance
Interior Design
International Business
Journalism
Laser Technology
Law

Law Enforcement and Criminal Justice
Library and Information Science
Machine Trades
Magazine Publishing
Management
Marine & Maritime
Marketing
Materials Science
Mechanical Engineering
Medical Technology
Metalworking
Microelectronics
Military
Modeling
Music
Newspaper Publishing
Nursing
Nutrition
Occupational Therapy
Office Occupations
Opticianry
Optometry
Packaging Science
Paralegal Careers
Paramedical Careers
Part-time & Summer Jobs
Performing Arts
Petroleum
Pharmacy
Photography
Physical Therapy
Physician
Plastics
Plumbing & Pipe Fitting
Podiatric Medicine
Postal Service
Printing
Property Management
Psychiatry
Psychology
Public Health
Public Relations
Purchasing
Real Estate
Recreation and Leisure
Refrigeration and Air Conditioning
Religious Service
Restaurant
Retailing
Robotics
Sales
Sales & Marketing
Secretarial
Securities
Social Science
Social Work
Speech-Language Pathology
Sports & Athletics
Sports Medicine
State and Local Government
Teaching
Technical Communications
Telecommunications
Television and Video
Theatrical Design & Production
Transportation
Travel
Trucking
Veterinary Medicine
Visual Arts
Vocational and Technical
Warehousing
Waste Management
Welding
Word Processing
Writing
Your Own Service Business

CAREERS IN Accounting; Advertising;
Business; Communications; Computers;
Education; Engineering; Health Care;
High Tech; Law; Marketing; Medicine;
Science

CAREER DIRECTORIES
Careers Encyclopedia
Dictionary of Occupational Titles
Occupational Outlook Handbook

CAREER PLANNING
Admissions Guide to Selective
  Business Schools
Career Planning and Development for
  College Students and Recent
  Graduates
Careers Checklists
Careers for Animal Lovers
Careers for Bookworms
Careers for Culture Lovers
Careers for Foreign Language
  Aficionados
Careers for Good Samaritans
Careers for Gourmets
Careers for Nature Lovers
Careers for Numbers Crunchers
Careers for Sports Nuts
Careers for Travel Buffs
Guide to Basic Resume Writing
Handbook of Business and
  Management Careers
Handbook of Health Care Careers
Handbook of Scientific and
  Technical Careers
How to Change Your Career
How to Choose the Right Career
How to Get and Keep
  Your First Job
How to Get into the Right Law School
How to Get People to Do Things
  Your Way
How to Have a Winning Job Interview
How to Land a Better Job
How to Make the Right Career Moves
How to Market Your College Degree
How to Prepare a *Curriculum Vitae*
How to Prepare for College
How to Run Your Own Home Business
How to Succeed in Collge
How to Succeed in High School
How to Write a Winning Resume
Joyce Lain Kennedy's Career Book
Planning Your Career of Tomorrow
Planning Your College Education
Planning Your Military Career
Planning Your Young Child's
  Education
Resumes for Advertising Careers
Resumes for College Students & Recent
  Graduates
Resumes for Communications Careers
Resumes for Education Careers
Resumes for High School Graduates
Resumes for High Tech Careers
Resumes for Sales and Marketing Careers
Successful Interviewing for College
  Seniors

SURVIVAL GUIDES
Dropping Out or Hanging In
High School Survival Guide
College Survival Guide

VGM Career Horizons
a division of *NTC Publishing Group*
4255 West Touhy Avenue
Lincolnwood, Illinois 60646-1975